D0733576

NOTE: This map, which has been prepared solely for the convenience of readers, does not purport to express political boundaries or relationships. The scale is a composite of several forms of projection.

DEMOGRAPHIC EFFECTS OF ECONOMIC REVERSALS IN SUB-SAHARAN AFRICA

• • • • • • • • • • • • • • •

Working Group on Demographic Effects of
Economic and Social Reversals

Panel on the Population Dynamics of Sub-Saharan Africa

Committee on Population

Commission on Behavioral and Social Sciences and Education

National Research Council

NATIONAL ACADEMY PRESS
Washington, D.C.   1993

NATIONAL ACADEMY PRESS • 2101 Constitution Avenue, N.W. • Washington, DC 20418

NOTICE: The project that is the subject of this report was approved by the Governing Board of the National Research Council, whose members are drawn from the councils of the National Academy of Sciences, the National Academy of Engineering, and the Institute of Medicine. The members of the committee responsible for the report were chosen for their special competences and with regard for appropriate balance.

This report has been reviewed by a group other than the authors according to procedures approved by a Report Review Committee consisting of members of the National Academy of Sciences, the National Academy of Engineering, and the Institute of Medicine.

The National Academy of Sciences is a private, nonprofit, self-perpetuating society of distinguished scholars engaged in scientific and engineering research, dedicated to the furtherance of science and technology and to their use for the general welfare. Upon the authority of the charter granted to it by the Congress in 1863, the Academy has a mandate that requires it to advise the federal government on scientific and technical matters. Dr. Frank Press is president of the National Academy of Sciences.

The National Academy of Engineering was established in 1964, under the charter of the National Academy of Sciences, as a parallel organization of outstanding engineers. It is autonomous in its administration and in the selection of its members, sharing with the National Academy of Sciences the responsibility for advising the federal government. The National Academy of Engineering also sponsors engineering programs aimed at meeting national needs, encourages education and research, and recognizes the superior achievements of engineers. Dr. Robert M. White is president of the National Academy of Engineering.

The Institute of Medicine was established in 1970 by the National Academy of Sciences to secure the services of eminent members of appropriate professions in the examination of policy matters pertaining to the health of the public. The Institute acts under the responsibility given to the National Academy of Sciences by its congressional charter to be an adviser to the federal government and, upon its own initiative, to identify issues of medical care, research, and education. Dr. Kenneth I. Shine is president of the Institute of Medicine.

The National Research Council was organized by the National Academy of Sciences in 1916 to associate the broad community of science and technology with the Academy's purposes of furthering knowledge and advising the federal government. Functioning in accordance with general policies determined by the Academy, the Council has become the principal operating agency of both the National Academy of Sciences and the National Academy of Engineering in providing services to the government, the public, and the scientific and engineering communities. The Council is administered jointly by both Academies and the Institute of Medicine. Dr. Frank Press and Dr. Robert M. White are chairman and vice chairman, respectively, of the National Research Council.

Library of Congress Catalog Card No. 93-84259
International Standard Book Number 0-309-04898-2

Additional copies of this report are available from: National Academy Press, 2101 Constitution Ave., N.W., Box 285, Washington, D.C. 20055. Call 800-624-6242 or 202-334-3313 (in the Washington Metropolitan Area).

B148

Printed in the United States of America

---

*through December 1991

v

Preface

This report is one in a series of studies that have been carried out under the auspices of the Panel on the Population Dynamics of Sub-Saharan Africa of the National Research Council's Committee on Population. The Research Council has a long history of examining population issues in developing countries. In 1971 it issued the report *Rapid Population Growth: Consequences and Policy Implications*. In 1977, the predecessor Committee on Population and Demography, began a major study of levels and trends of fertility and mortality in the developing world that resulted in 13 country reports and 6 reports on demographic methods. Then, in the early 1980s, it undertook a study of the determinants of fertility in the developing world, which resulted in 10 reports. In the mid- and late-1980s, the Committee on Population assessed the economic consequences of population growth and the health consequences of contraceptive use and controlled fertility, among many other activities.

No publication on the demography of sub-Saharan Africa emerged from the early work of the committee, largely because of the paucity of data and the poor quality of what was available. However, the censuses, ethnographic studies, and surveys of recent years, such as those under the auspices of the World Fertility Survey and the Demographic and Health Survey Programs, have made available data on the demography of sub-Saharan Africa. The data collection has no doubt been stimulated by the increasing interest of both scholars and policymakers in the demographic development of Africa and the relations between demographic change and socioeconomic developments. In response to this interest, the Committee on Population held a meeting in 1989 to ascertain the feasibility and desirability of a major study of the demography of Africa, and decided to set up a Panel on the Population Dynamics of Sub-Saharan Africa.

The panel, which is chaired by Kenneth Hill and includes members from Africa, Europe, and the United States, met for the first time in February 1990 in Washington, D.C. At that meeting the panel decided to set up six working groups, composed of its own members and other experts on the demography of Africa, to carry out specific studies. Four working groups focused on cross-national studies of substantive issues: the social dynamics of adolescent fertility, factors affecting contraceptive use, the effects on mortality of child survival and general health programs, and the demographic effects of economic reversals. The two other working groups were charged with in-depth studies of Kenya and Senegal, with the objective of studying linkages between demographic variables and between those variables and socioeconomic changes. The panel also decided to publish a volume of papers reviewing levels and trends of fertility, nuptiality, the proximate determinants of fertility, child mortality, adult mortality, internal migration, and international migration, as well as the demographic consequences of the AIDS epidemic.

This report, one of the four cross-national studies, analyzes the short-run demographic effects of economic reversals and, in particular, the responses to changes in economic conditions of child mortality, timing of first marriages, and timing of first and second births. It focuses on the demographic and economic experiences in recent decades of seven countries: Botswana, Ghana, Kenya, Nigeria, Senegal, Togo, and Uganda. These countries were selected not because they are necessarily representative of sub-Saharan Africa, but because they exhibited a variety of economic structures and histories; moreover, each was recently the subject of a survey under the auspices of the Demographic and Health Survey Program.

In doing the analysis, the most sophisticated multivariate techniques that the data would bear have been used. Nevertheless, an attempt has been made to make the report accessible to a nontechnical audience. The technical discussion is confined to Chapter 4, which reviews the methods used, and to the two appendixes, which describe the sources of the economic and demographic data.

As is the case for all of the panel's work, this report would not have been possible without the cooperation and assistance of the Demographic and Health Survey (DHS) Program of the Institute for Resource Development/Macro Systems. We are grateful to the DHS staff for responding to our inquiries and facilitating our early access to the survey data.

We are also grateful to the organizations that provided financial support for the work of the panel: the Office of Population and the Africa Bureau of the Agency for International Development, the Andrew W. Mellon Foundation, the William and Flora Hewlett Foundation, and the Rockefeller Foundation. Besides providing funding, the representatives of these organizations were a source of information and advice in the development of the panel's overall work plan.

This report results from the joint efforts of the working group members and staff and represents a consensus of the members' views on the issues addressed. The Committee on Population and the Panel on the Population Dynamics of Sub-Saharan Africa appreciate the time and energy that all the working group members devoted to the study. Several members and others deserve recognition for their special contributions: George Adansi-Pipim, Laurent Assogba, and Jackson Mukiza-Gapere played key roles in obtaining documents on their respective countries, Ghana, Togo, and Uganda, and in the understanding of the experiences there. Mukiza-Gapere also graciously hosted the second of the three meetings of the working group at Makerere University in Kampala. Catherine Hill kindly provided economic data on Botswana. Andrew Foster carried out the analysis of marriage and fertility with assistance from Pierre Ngom of the University of Pennsylvania, and Kenneth Hill and Linda Martin undertook the analysis of child mortality with the assistance of Ghulam Soomro of Johns Hopkins University. Foster also wrote the first draft of Chapter 3; Hill, of Chapters 1 and 6; and Martin, of Chapters 4 and 7 and the demographic portions of Chapters 2 and 5. Christina Paxson compiled the time series of economic data used in the analysis and wrote the first drafts of the economic portions of Chapters 2 and 5. Martin served as the principal editor and coordinator of the final manuscript.

Special thanks are also due Susan Coke and Diane Goldman for providing superb administrative and logistical support to the working group, to Mendelle T. Berenson and Florence Poillon for skillful editing of the report, to Elaine McGarraugh for her meticulous production assistance, and to Eugenia Grohman for valuable guidance and extraordinary patience through the review and production processes.

SAMUEL H. PRESTON, *Chair*
Committee on Population

Contents

Executive Summary

This report stems from concern that the economic decline in some sub-Saharan African countries in the last 15 years may have especially affected the welfare of vulnerable groups, such as children. Historical evidence from preindustrial Europe suggests that demographic phenomena—mortality, marriage, and childbearing—are linked to changes in economic conditions over time. Our task is to ascertain whether such relationships hold in the short term for contemporary sub-Saharan Africa.

DIVERSITY OF ECONOMIC EXPERIENCES

The experiences of seven countries—Botswana, Ghana, Kenya, Nigeria, Senegal, Togo, and Uganda—are analyzed in this report. Although not representative of all of sub-Saharan Africa, these countries were chosen to reflect the diversity of African economic experience. Following a pattern that is fairly typical of the "average" African country, Kenya, Nigeria, and Togo had moderate to high economic growth rates in the 1970s and negative rates of growth in the 1980s. Ghana's economic performance began to deteriorate in the mid-1970s, and Uganda experienced a sharp decline in the 1970s. Senegal's economy has not grown at all in recent decades, while Botswana's has grown steadily. All seven countries, however, rely heavily on primary commodity exports for their incomes, and all experienced adverse movements in their terms of trade in the 1980s.

1

DATA AND METHODOLOGY

To analyze the effects of economic reversals on demographic outcomes we would ideally use long time series of demographic events. However, vital registration systems in sub-Saharan Africa are limited in coverage and thus do not provide the necessary numbers. To construct time series of events, we rely instead on retrospective reports of individual women about their marriages and the births and deaths of their children. The data we use are drawn from the nationally representative Demographic and Health Surveys (DHS) that were conducted in each of our seven study countries sometime in the period 1986-1990. The demographic outcomes that we are able to analyze using the DHS data are first marriages, first births, second births, and deaths of children under age 5.

To measure economic conditions over time, we use the following indicators for each country where available: gross domestic product per capita, the quantity of exports, terms of trade, and world and producer prices of commodities that are important to each country. Not available to us were time series of information on income distribution or public expenditures on social, health, and family planning programs. We do not attempt to link economic conditions to the implementation of structural adjustment programs.

We estimate the effects, both current and lagged, of macroeconomic indicators on the occurrence of the demographic events by fitting multivariate hazard models that also control for linear time trends. We analyze first marriages and first and second births from the first part of the 1960s to the second part of the 1980s, the precise years depending on the survey date in each country. We analyze child mortality from 1970 to the mid- to late-1980s. Where possible, we fit separate models for urban and rural populations.

HYPOTHESES

If economic reversals have demographic effects, then we expect economic downturns to be associated with below-trend probabilities of marriage and fertility and above-trend mortality rates. Depending on economic and political factors, we also expect the effects in urban and rural areas to differ. For example, governments that attempt to protect domestic producer prices from variation in world prices may have to restrict public services as they adjust to lower world prices. If public services generally benefit urban more than rural populations, the effects of economic reversals should be greater in urban areas. Finally, we expect stronger effects in economies dominated by one commodity and experiencing an especially strong economic shock.

FINDINGS

We find that the effects of poor economic conditions on child mortality net of trend are clearest for Ghana (especially in rural areas) and Nigeria (especially in urban areas). The positive association between economic conditions and the odds of marrying for the first time is also quite clear in Botswana, Senegal, and Togo (especially in urban areas). The results for first births are the strongest of the results for the four demographic outcomes. In all seven countries, except Kenya, there is a consistently positive relation to economic variation net of trend. On the other hand, the results for second births are perhaps the weakest. Only for Botswana, Ghana, and Uganda do we find consistently positive relations between second births and economic conditions.

Nigeria stands out as the country with the strongest across-the-board effects of economic reversals. We believe that the dominance of one commodity, oil, in the economy and the severity of the economic shock account for this finding. In contrast, relatively few effects appeared in Kenya, which did not suffer so severe a shock and whose economy is not so dependent upon one commodity.

Our analysis is subject to many caveats and the estimated effects vary in size and pattern, especially depending on the economic indicator used in the model. Nevertheless, we conclude that the economic reversals experienced in sub-Saharan Africa have indeed had demographic effects and that the lives of many Africans have been affected as they suffered the deaths of their children and made decisions to delay or forgo marriage and parenthood.

1

Introduction

The 1980s was a decade of economic stagnation or reversal for much of sub-Saharan Africa. For the region as a whole, real gross national product (GNP) per capita declined between 1980 and 1987 at an annual rate of 2.8 percent, and for the region's low-income countries (per capita GNP less then $500 in 1987), fell at an annual rate of 3.6 percent (World Bank, 1989b). Economic performance in other parts of the developing world over the same period was mixed: Per capita real gross national product grew at an annual rate of 4.0 percent for all low-income countries, but declined at an annual rate of 1.1 percent when China and India are excluded.

Various explanations have been put forward for the poor performance of many developing country economies in the 1980s. These explanations, discussed in more detail in Chapter 2, generally incorporate one or more of these factors: one, adverse trends during the 1980s in world commodity prices, which reduced export revenues and returns to producers; two, excessive levels of (mainly public) debt owed to foreign banks and governments, which constrained the external sector with high foreign exchange outlays; and three, excessive government interference in the economy, through both state monopolies and other regulation. Some have also argued that poor performance has been exacerbated by remedial policies, often called structural adjustment programs, that have been imposed by organizations such as the International Monetary Fund and the World Bank and that are intended to eliminate inefficiencies in the economy.

As the magnitude of the recession in developing countries became evident in the early 1980s, institutions and individuals raised concerns about the effects on vulnerable groups. Particularly influential was a volume published in 1984 under the auspices of the United Nations International Children's Emergency Fund, *The Impact of World Recession on Children* (Jolly and Cornia, 1984). The underlying argument of this volume was that the recession, and especially the adjustment policies introduced in the name of sound economic management, adversely affected the welfare of the young. Two subsequent volumes of essays and country case studies (Cornia et al., 1987, 1989) reviewed theoretical mechanisms through which the effects might operate and included preliminary evidence that adjustment policies had been associated with increases in infant and child mortality in some of the countries studied.

Links between the economic and demographic parameters of a population are intuitively plausible. In the case of mortality, the association seems clear. On a cross-sectional basis, high-income countries have lower mortality, whatever indicator is chosen, than low-income countries. Similarly, from a longitudinal perspective, gains in life expectancy and falls in child mortality have in general accompanied gains in per capita income. For fertility, the cross-sectional and longitudinal relationships suggest that income gains are associated with lower fertility, though the short-term response is probably the opposite. The third component of population change, migration, is more complex. It is generally seen as driven partly by real wage differentials between origins and destinations, but also by the costs of migration, so that a surprising positive relationship with economic conditions in the place of origin emerges.

Attempts have been made to follow up on the preliminary UNICEF findings in contemporary developing country settings and to test rigorously the hypothesis that economic reversals have demographic effects. As Chapter 3 describes in greater detail, there is a body of knowledge on the relationships between economic conditions and demographic parameters, particularly in historical populations. However, despite the clear associations between long-term economic and demographic changes, establishing any causal relationship between them has been extremely difficult partly because of the complexity of the processes involved and partly because of the impossibility of setting up true experimental tests.

Short-term relationships have proven more tractable. Extensive analysis of time-series data for preindustrial Europe reveals persistent and plausible demographic responses to economic conditions, and limited work in the contemporary developing world suggests similar links. However, as the discussion in Chapter 3 shows, few systematic studies of the effects of the 1980s recession have been carried out, except for Latin America. As a result, the Committee on Population's Panel on Population Dynamics of Sub-Saharan Africa decided to undertake a major initiative in this area as a part of its work program. A working group was established to review the literature and to utilize existing data sets to explore links between demographic outcomes and a variety of economic indicators that capture different dimensions of the recession. The underlying strategy has been to use retrospective event history data as a substitute for vital registration data to provide annual series of risks of demographic events that can be related to annual series of economic measures with suitable lags. The focus is not on structural adjustment per se, but on general economic conditions.

A review of economic and demographic change in sub-Saharan Africa is presented in Chapter 2. The sources of economic data, their limitations, and definitions of the economic variables used in the study can be found in Appendix A. A discussion of the conceptual framework is presented in Chapter 3 and the methodology in Chapter 4.

The demographic data that we use come from the Demographic and Health Survey (DHS) Program. Nationally representative surveys under this program have been carried out in a dozen countries of sub-Saharan Africa. The surveys follow a standardized format, with information collected from all women concerning date of first marriage, and dates of birth and, if relevant, age at death, of all children ever born alive. The nature of the data limits the demographic outcomes that can be studied. No information is available on the mortality of adults, so we only examine child mortality risks. However, such risks have been the focus of many of the concerns raised about economic crisis. The surveys do not include complete marriage histories, recording only date of first marriage, so we can only study first marriage rates. We also limit analysis of fertility to first and second births, because the numbers of births decline rapidly as birth order rises, and because of the severe conditionality constraints applied to higher-order births (for example, only a woman who already has had exactly two births can have a third). However, in the absence of widespread contraceptive use, family formation and initiation of childbearing are important determinants of overall fertility and population growth. Because migration histories are not available from the DHS, we cannot study the link between economic variation and migration risks. A discussion of the DHS and the quality of data can be found in Appendix B.

Nor have we analyzed all the available surveys for sub-Saharan Africa. Rather, we have tried to include in our analysis countries that represent different types of economic experience—Botswana, Ghana, Kenya, Nigeria, Senegal, Togo, and Uganda. We chose these countries not because their populations and economic experiences represent all of Africa. Rather, the aim was to choose countries that reflect the diversity of African experience (and for which data from a Demographic and Health Survey were available). The countries are located in eastern Africa (Kenya and Uganda), southern Africa (Botswana), and western Africa (Ghana, Nigeria, Senegal, and Togo). The recent economic and demographic histories of these countries are broadly described in Chapter 2. The results of the analysis for each of the seven countries, along with in-depth discussions of their recent economic histories, are presented in Chapter 5. Chapter 6 compares the results across countries, and Chapter 7 presents caveats and conclusions.

2

Economic and Demographic Overview of Sub-Saharan Africa and the Seven Countries Studied

This chapter presents an overview of the economy and demography of sub-Saharan Africa, as a background for the examination of the relation between the two in the seven countries selected for study here. It first outlines the economic changes in the region as a whole, and then takes up the economic changes in the seven countries. Next, it reviews the demographic changes in both the region and the seven countries.

ECONOMIC CHANGE IN SUB-SAHARAN AFRICA

The economies of many sub-Saharan African countries have performed poorly during the past 15 years.[1]   Although many of these experienced moderate, steady rates of growth in the 1960s and early 1970s, these rates tended to decline in the later 1970s and to decline even further in the 1980s. The average annual rate of growth of real gross national product per capita for all sub-Saharan countries was −2.8 percent from 1980 to 1987, in contrast with rates of 2.9 percent from 1965 to 1973 and of 0.1 percent from 1973 to 1980 (World Bank, 1989b).   Moreover, African countries fared worse than other developing countries in the 1980s. For example, the average annual rate of growth of real gross national product per capita between 1980 and 1987 was 4.0 percent for all low-income countries, as classified by the World Bank, in contrast with −3.6 percent for all low-income African

---

[1]In what follows, "Africa" means sub-Saharan Africa, including all African countries except South Africa, Namibia, Egypt, Libya, Tunisia, Algeria, and Morocco.

countries. For some African countries, average standards of living were lower in 1987 than they had been in the 1960s.

These aggregate statistics mask considerable diversity among African countries. Not all African countries followed the "typical" pattern of high to moderate growth in the 1960s and 1970s and decline in the 1980s. One group of countries, including Botswana and Cameroon, continued to grow rapidly in the 1980s. Another group, including Uganda, Chad, and Angola, experienced large declines in living standards during the 1970s, mainly due to political instability. The economies of others, such as Benin and Senegal, have simply been stagnant over the past several decades.

Still, the general pattern for African countries in the 1980s is one of decline. Furthermore, several factors stand out as at least partially responsible for this decline. First, the economies of most African countries rely heavily on exports of primary commodities, whose prices were typically low during the 1980s relative to the 1960s and 1970s (see Gersovitz and Paxson, 1990). For many African countries, declines in commodity prices produced declines in the terms of trade (prices of exports relative to the prices of imports) for many African countries. For example, of the 29 African countries for which the United Nations Committee on Trade and Development reports terms of trade, only 3 had terms of trade that were higher in 1982-1985 than in 1974-1979, and only 10 had terms of trade that were higher than in 1960-1973 (Gersovitz and Paxson, 1990). These declines meant reductions in export earnings and purchasing power for a large group of African countries.

Second, the decline in commodity prices provoked a debt crisis for many African countries. These countries had increased their indebtedness during the 1970s and early 1980s. Public and publicly guaranteed obligations for payments of principal and interest to foreign lenders (external public debt service obligations) rose from 1.2 percent of gross national product (GNP) in 1970 to 4.1 percent in 1987; and for every sub-Saharan African country with available data, debt as a fraction of GNP was higher in 1987 than in 1980 (World Bank, 1989b). The decline in commodity prices, and the resulting loss in export earnings, made it increasingly difficult for many African countries to meet their debt service obligations that represented an increasingly large share of export earnings. For example, between 1985 and 1988, debt service actually paid accounted for 27 percent of African export earnings (World Bank, 1989b). Some countries ceased making debt payments, a move that enabled them to retain their export earnings but hampered them in obtaining new foreign lending.

Foreign aid to African countries generally increased in the 1980s and may have partially offset the effects of adverse movements in export earnings for some countries. Total official development assistance per sub-Saharan African person increased (in nominal terms) from $20 to $25 between 1980 and 1987 (World Bank, 1989b). However, both the level of aid received and the size of increases in aid in the 1980s varied widely across countries. For example, the reported level of foreign aid in 1980 was $0 per person in Nigeria, in contrast to $118 in Botswana. In general, aid levels and average living standards have no clear relationship. For example, the average level of development assistance per person was larger for middle-income African countries than for low-income African countries (World Bank, 1989b). Furthermore, the countries that experienced the steepest declines in living standards in the 1980s were not necessarily the countries that received the greatest increases in foreign assistance. For example, nominal official development assistance to Nigeria rose from $0 per person to $1 per person between 1980 and 1987, hardly enough to offset declines in real per capita GNP that averaged 4.8 percent per year in that same period (World Bank, 1989b).

Although many African countries clearly suffered slow or negative growth in the 1980s, little direct evidence bears on how this recession affected the incomes of different groups of people within countries. Few African countries systematically collect data on income distribution, and none has reliable data on how the incomes of different groups of people have changed over time. Furthermore, the available evidence suggests that the recession affected these countries in widely varying ways, depending on the source and severity of the decline, as well as on the responses of individual governments.

One common feature of the 1980s recession was its adverse effect on the revenues of African governments. These governments rely heavily on direct and indirect trade taxes for their revenues (see Gersovitz and Paxson, 1990). This reliance is especially great for countries that export metals and minerals. For example, in 1985 the Nigerian government retained 100 percent of export earnings, and oil export earnings accounted for 73 percent of the total taxes it received. Two-thirds of government revenues in the Congo in the late 1980s were derived from oil exports (Central Intelligence Agency, 1989). Likewise, 73 percent of the tax revenues of the Botswana government in 1987-1988 were derived from minerals, mostly diamonds (unpublished national accounts data). In virtually all African countries, the government is either the sole or the majority owner of mining companies (U.S. Department of Interior, 1984). For countries that rely on mineral exports, declines in mineral prices and thus in profits of mining companies inevitably mean direct declines in government revenues.

Many governments also rely on direct and indirect taxes on agricultural commodities for revenue. However, the declines in the prices of these commodities affect government revenues differently from country to country, depending on the producer pricing policies the governments follow. Some countries, such as Kenya and Sierra Leone, impose ad valorem taxes on agricultural exports. In this case, although government revenues decline with export prices, so do revenues of private producers and by a similar percentage. Other countries, such as Côte d'Ivoire and Togo, have sought to stabilize the prices that farmers receive for their products by maintaining producer prices that do not fluctuate as much as world prices. In this case, reductions in the world price of the commodity result largely in reductions in government revenues, leaving producers' incomes relatively stable (see Gersovitz and Paxson, 1990).

African countries have responded in very different ways to the erosion in government revenues. For example, when Nigerian revenues collapsed with oil prices in the early 1980s, the government initially attempted to maintain government expenditures through deficit financing. Later attempts to reduce the deficit included across-the-board spending cuts. Urban unemployment rose, and public health and education systems deteriorated. Other countries have been more successful at maintaining stable living standards despite shocks to the economy. The Botswana government, for example, has responded to fluctuations in diamond revenues by building up and drawing down financial reserves, thereby protecting living standards (see Hill and Mokgethi, 1989). Countries have differed as well in the types of expenditures they attempt to maintain in the face of declining revenues. In a study of how governments of African and non-African developing countries cut expenditures, Hicks and Kubisch (1984) conclude that governments generally tend to protect current expenditures more than capital expenditures, and social, administrative, and defense expenditures more than those on infrastructure and other production activities. However, they note countries vary widely in the amount of protection they give to different categories of expenditures.

Despite this diversity, several general trends are apparent in the expenditure data. First, according to some evidence, in many African countries government expenditures on health declined in the 1980s. In six of the ten low-income African countries for which data are available, the fraction of GNP allocated to government expenditures on health declined between 1980 and 1987 (World Bank, 1989b). In each of the six, real income per capita also declined, so that health expenditures per person shrank. This was true even for Liberia, one of the four countries that reported increases in the share of GNP allocated to health expenditures, because it had such a large reduction in real GNP per capita.

The link between health expenditures and economic conditions for the seven countries studied in this report is illustrated by time-series data from 1975 to 1985 in Figure 2-1. Despite the similarity in patterns of change over time, real per capita expenditures on health care by governments may be an inadequate measure of the provision of health care services (Ogbu and Gallagher, 1992). In particular, these authors note that countries often re-

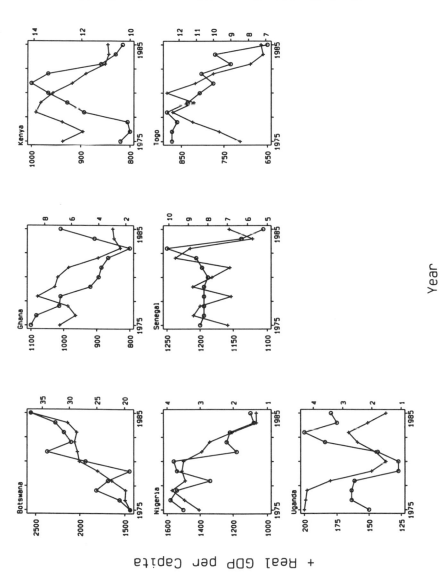

FIGURE 2-1 Real gross domestic product and real health expenditures per capita, 1975-1985, seven study countries.
SOURCES: Gross domestic product data, Appendix A; health expenditure data, Ogbu and Gal:agher (1992).

duce health care expenditures inefficiently, for example, cutting expenditures on essential drugs while maintaining payrolls, thus exacerbating the adverse effects of budget cuts.

Second, as evidence from the International Labour Organization indicates, for many African countries, real wages of modern and public sector employees declined during the 1980s. Furthermore, wages apparently have become more compressed, falling the most for those at the upper end of the pay scale (see Vandemoortele, 1991, for a summary). Also, open unemployment rates rose over the same period. In some instances, declines in export prices (often for metals and minerals) prompted governments to reduce wages and employment levels in the export sector. When, for example, copper prices declined during the 1970s and early 1980s, the Zambian government reduced the real wage paid to copper miners 53 percent between 1970 and 1984 and cut employment in mining as well (International Labour Organization, various years). Many countries responded to low government revenues by holding annual increases in the wages of civil servants far below rates of inflation. For example, between 1975 and 1983, real basic starting salaries of Ghanaian civil servants fell by 60 to 90 percent, depending on the type of job (Lindauer et al., 1988).

This sketchy evidence suggests that the recession of the 1980s lowered the living standards of many Africans. What we do not know, because reliable data are lacking, is how the declines were distributed within countries. More than 70 percent of the African labor force is employed in agriculture, and more than 70 percent of the total African population lives in rural areas. Direct evidence on the living standards of these individuals, and how living standards changed during the 1980s, is especially scarce. Rural living standards depend on many factors, including the prices producers receive for their crops, the prices they pay for inputs, wages and employment prospects in rural labor markets, public investment in rural infrastructure, access to publicly provided health and human services, and weather conditions. For many countries, only the prices that producers receive for exports crops are available, and so we have relied on them as crude measures of rural living standards. Of course, not everyone is employed in producing these crops, but changes in their prices may have spillover effects on prices, wages, and employment related to the production of other crops.

ECONOMIC EXPERIENCE OF THE SEVEN STUDY COUNTRIES

This study uses data from seven countries to examine whether and how economic changes over the past several decades affected demographic outcomes. The seven countries we have selected are Botswana, Ghana, Kenya,

Nigeria, Senegal, Togo, and Uganda. Appendix A provides details on the economic data sources and definitions, as well as the time series used in the analysis.

As Table 2-1 shows, these countries have very different per capita incomes. In 1980, real gross domestic product (GDP) per capita in Botswana (the richest country in our sample) was 7.8 times that of Uganda (the poorest). The patterns of growth between 1960 and the late 1980s also varied across these countries, as Table 2-1 and Figure 2-2 reveal. Senegal experienced almost no growth, Botswana grew steadily, and Ghana began to deteriorate markedly in the mid-1970s. Kenya, Nigeria, and Togo followed the pattern that is more typical of the "average" African country; they had moderate to high growth rates in the 1970s and negative growth rates in the 1980s. Uganda experienced a sharp decline in the 1970s.

Whatever their differences, these seven countries are similar to each other (and to other African countries) in their heavy reliance on exports of primary commodities for their incomes, and in the deterioration in their terms of trade in the 1980s. Table 2-2 documents the importance of primary commodity exports to each of the seven countries in 1984, and patterns in export quantities and in the terms of trade in the 1974-1985 time period (relative to 1960-1973 values).[2] It highlights several important factors. First, the countries with the lowest fractions of exports in GNP in 1984, Ghana and Uganda, have experienced fairly dramatic reductions in their export quantities since the 1960-1973 time period. Their currently low reliance on exports does not necessarily mean, however, that changes in export conditions have not been important determinants of economic performance.

Second, in all but one of the six countries for which data on terms of trade are available, terms of trade deteriorated between 1974-1979 and 1982-1985. (And even the exception, Nigeria, an oil exporter, experienced a decline in its terms of trade between 1980-1981 and 1982-1985.) However, for only two countries—Ghana and Kenya—were terms of trade worse in 1982-1985 than in 1960-1973. For four of the seven countries, the 1980s saw simply the end of a boom in their terms of trade, rather than unprecedented low levels. In this respect, these seven countries have not all experienced the continuous decline that many other African countries have, as discussed earlier.

Another way of analyzing changes in the international economic environment of these seven countries is to look directly at the real prices of the commodities each exports. As Table 2-3 shows, each relies on a few pri-

---

[2]Note that indices of the terms of trade (and export quantities) in all subperiods are expressed relative to average values for 1960-1973. For example, the first row of Table 2-2 indicates that terms of trade in Ghana in 1982-1985 were 81 percent of average 1960-1973 values.

TABLE 2-1   Real Gross Domestic Product per Capita as a Fraction of
1980 Gross Domestic Product per Capita, Seven Sub-Saharan African
Countries

Year	Botswana	Ghana	Kenya	Nigeria	Senegal	Togo	Uganda
1960	0.254	1.053	0.613	0.634	0.974	0.488	—
1961	0.266	1.085	0.540	0.610	0.992	0.477	1.642
1962	0.279	1.084	0.562	0.610	1.032	0.491	1.562
1963	0.285	1.093	0.591	0.644	1.062	0.485	1.555
1964	0.295	1.066	0.614	0.667	1.063	0.554	1.606
1965	0.274	1.069	0.613	0.671	1.067	0.655	1.547
1966	0.286	1.037	0.659	0.622	1.072	0.655	1.577
1967	0.345	1.055	0.679	0.518	1.048	0.706	1.591
1968	0.386	1.064	0.705	0.511	1.053	0.708	1.577
1969	0.392	1.101	0.727	0.625	0.939	0.751	1.701
1970	0.480	1.151	0.744	0.767	0.986	0.766	1.657
1971	0.486	1.172	0.925	0.858	0.975	0.759	1.635
1972	0.543	1.139	1.020	0.871	0.982	0.795	1.613
1973	0.648	1.099	0.976	0.901	0.929	0.801	1.591
1974	0.745	1.156	1.000	0.981	0.932	0.828	1.569
1975	0.718	0.994	0.979	0.938	0.980	0.807	1.460
1976	0.746	0.947	0.936	0.995	1.024	0.861	1.453
1977	0.743	0.970	0.980	1.047	1.015	0.932	1.445
1978	0.820	1.061	1.037	0.993	0.975	0.984	1.314
1979	0.898	1.009	1.026	1.006	1.025	0.929	1.080
1980	1.000	1.000	1.000	1.000	1.000	1.000	1.000
1981	1.010	0.968	0.959	0.928	0.977	0.925	1.058
1982	1.026	0.880	0.930	0.896	1.047	0.877	1.160
1983	1.014	0.814	0.889	0.805	1.028	0.781	1.212
1984	1.066	0.833	0.882	0.710	0.949	0.747	1.102
1985	1.273	0.837	0.884	0.711	0.978	0.752	1.000
1986	1.137	0.840	0.902	0.705	0.938	0.787	0.912
1987	—	0.859	0.924	0.662	0.943	0.744	0.920
1988	—	0.871	0.947	0.664	0.950	0.743	—
Real GDP per capita, 1980 (1985 U.S. dollars)	2,007	1,018	956	1,499	1,182	884	258

SOURCES: All numbers, except for Uganda, are drawn from the Penn World Tables (Mark
5); see Summers and Heston (1991) for a description of these data. For these countries, real
per capita GDP is calculated using a Laspeyres index. For Uganda, data are from United
Nations Development Program/World Bank (1989). See Appendix A for a discussion of
problems with the Ugandan numbers.

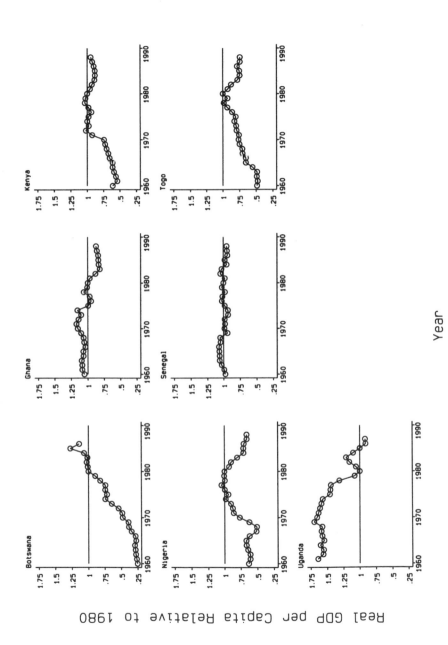

FIGURE 2-2 Real gross domestic product per capita relative to 1980, 1960 to late 1980s, seven study countries.
SOURCE: Table 2-1.

TABLE 2-2 Exports and Terms of Trade, Seven Sub-Saharan African Countries

Country	Exports as Percentage of GNP, 1984	Export Quantum as Percentage of Average 1960-1973 Values			Terms of Trade as Percentage of Average 1960-1973 Values		
		1974-1979	1980-1981	1982-1985	1974-1979	1980-1981	1982-1985
Botswana[a]	.63	—	—	—	—	—	—
Ghana	.11	78	71	60	150	106	81
Kenya	.26	106	90	79	113	93	90
Nigeria	.16	161	123	87	332	583	526
Senegal	.29	91	71	92	159	112	101
Togo	.31	108	156	128	234	141	124
Uganda	.11	67	39	55	122	106	104

[a]Comparable data on Botswana are not available because the Botswana trade figures are not reported separately from the South African Customs Union.

SOURCES: For all countries except Botswana, data on exports as a fraction of GNP in 1984 are from World Bank (1986b). Data on exports as a fraction of GDP for Botswana are from unpublished national accounts data, kindly supplied by Catherine Hill. See Appendix A for a discussion of all other data and their sources.

TABLE 2-3 Shares of Commodities in Country's Total Exports (percent)

Country and Commodity	1966-1973	1974-1979	1980-1981	1982-1984
Botswana				
Diamonds	—	36	51	64
Copper-nickel matte	—	23	23	10
Meat	—	26	12	11
Total	—	85	86	85
Ghana				
Cocoa	55	60	56	57
Wood	11	8	3	3
Aluminum	8	8	20	
Total	74	76	79	60
Kenya				
Coffee	18	26	21	25
Petroleum products	12	19	32	22
Tea	11	12	11	19
Total	41	57	64	66
Nigeria				
Crude petroleum	52	92	96	100
Cocoa	14	4	2	2
Total	66	96	98	102[a]
Senegal				
Groundnuts	44	32	9	17
Phosphates	9	17	15	9
Petroleum products	3	9	23	19
Fish	7	11	21	17
Total	63	69	68	62
Togo				
Phosphates	39	58	46	51
Cocoa	30	19	13	15
Coffee	17	11	8	7
Petroleum products	—	4	14	1
Total	86	92	81	74
Uganda				
Coffee	50	85	99	92
Cotton	21	7	1	—
Total	71	92	100	92

NOTE: Only commodities that have substantially contributed to export earnings during the sample period are included.

[a]The sum greater than 100 is a statistical artifact.

SOURCES: For countries other than Botswana, the source of the data is the International Monetary Fund (1987); for Botswana, the source is unpublished government documents, supplied by Catherine Hill.

mary commodities for the bulk of its export earnings. For Botswana, Ghana, Nigeria, and Uganda, more than 50 percent of export earnings in the 1980s was derived from a single commodity (diamonds, cocoa, crude petroleum, and coffee, respectively). Kenya, Senegal, and Togo had more diverse export bases. However, the apparent reliance of these three countries on exports of petroleum products is misleading. Each imports crude petroleum and exports refined petroleum products. Movements in the price of crude petroleum have little effect on the terms of trade or purchasing power of these countries.

Table 2-4 presents average values of real commodity prices on the world market for a set of commodities exported by the seven countries. For all commodities, real prices declined in the 1980s relative to average 1974-1979 values. Four of the seven countries, Ghana, Kenya, Togo, and Uganda, rely heavily on exports of coffee or cocoa (or both), and prices of these two commodities plunged. The prices of phosphates (important to Senegal and Togo), groundnut oil (Senegal), and crude petroleum (Nigeria) also experienced booms in the 1970s and subsequent declines. Although a long time series on the price of diamonds, Botswana's major export, is not available, evidence from Hill and Mokgethi (1989) indicates that diamond prices rose markedly between 1977 and 1980, collapsed between 1980 and 1982, and then recovered between 1982 and 1985.

This section has focused on the changes in the international economic environment that affected the economic performance of these seven countries. These international factors, of course, are not the sole determinants of economic performance. Other factors, such as political stability and the

TABLE 2-4   Average Real Commodity Prices Relative to Sample Mean

	1950-1973	1974-1979	1980-1985	1986-1987
Cocoa	0.93	1.46	0.93	0.70
Coffee	0.95	1.33	0.93	0.78
Tea	1.20	0.76	0.68	0.44
Groundnut meal	1.14	0.92	0.69	0.47
Groundnut oil	1.06	1.20	0.78	0.41
Cotton	1.12	0.94	0.77	0.49
Crude petroleum	0.52	1.41	2.50	1.04
Phosphates	0.96	1.37	0.92	0.60

NOTES: All prices run from 1950 to 1987, except for tea (1951 to 1987). Real prices are computed as the nominal average price for the year, divided by the manufactures unit value (MUV) index, which is a general price index for exports of manufactured products from developed to developing countries. Average real commodity prices are divided by the sample mean for the full 1950-1987 period (or the period for which data are available). See Appendix A for a discussion of these data and their source.

soundness of economic policies, have been important as well. For some countries, particularly Uganda with its political turmoil, the international economic environment has arguably played only a minor role in the determination of living standards. Moreover, it could be that a relatively small proportion of the population is involved in producing export crops, or it could be that environmental factors, for example, rainfall, are more important in some settings than others. Unfortunately, when we did our analysis, we had access to such environmental data over time only for Senegal. In Chapter 5, we present more detailed descriptions of the economic performance and economic policies of each of these seven countries over the past several decades, to understand better how economic fluctuations may have affected demographic outcomes.

DEMOGRAPHIC CHANGE IN SUB-SAHARAN AFRICA AND THE SEVEN STUDY COUNTRIES

Because the Panel on the Population Dynamics of Sub-Saharan Africa has published a separate volume evaluating demographic levels and trends in the region (Panel on the Population Dynamics of Sub-Saharan Africa, 1993), the discussion here of these issues is brief and focuses primarily on the seven populations considered in this report.

In comparison to the rest of the world and even to other less developed regions, population growth rates remain high in sub-Saharan Africa. For eastern, middle, and western Africa, annual growth rates were estimated to be over 3.0 percent for 1985 to 1990, in comparison with 2.06 percent in Latin America and 1.87 percent in Asia (see Table 2-5). Rates over 3 percent imply a doubling of population in less than 25 years. The countries in our study include the most populous African country—Nigeria—with 87.5 million people as enumerated by the 1991 census, and one of the smallest—Botswana—with only 1 million.

Considerable progress has been made in reducing infant and child mortality in Africa in recent decades (Hill, 1993), although it has not been uniform. Of our seven countries, Kenya and Botswana have made the greatest progress so that their recent infant mortality rates are comparable with those in Latin America and Asia, as shown in Table 2-5. In Ghana and Uganda, mortality declines are thought to have stalled in the late 1970s and early 1980s.

Until recently, there was generally little expectation of near-term decline in fertility in Africa (see Caldwell and Caldwell, 1990). Now, evidence from the Demographic and Health Surveys (DHS; Institute for Resource Development, various years), which were conducted in the mid- to late-1980s, indicates that fertility has begun to fall in some countries. Most notable have been the declines in Botswana, Kenya, and Zimbabwe (Cohen,

TABLE 2-5 Demographic Indicators in Selected Regions of Africa and the World and in Seven Sub-Saharan African Countries

Region and Country	Population, 1985 (millions)	Population Growth Rate, 1985-1990[a] (percent)	Infant Mortality Rate, 1985-1990[a] (deaths per 1,000 births)	Total Fertility Rate (children per woman aged 15-49)	
				DHS, Mid- to Late-1980s	UN[a], 1985-1990
Eastern Africa	167.8	3.19	114	—	6.85
Kenya	20.1	3.58	72	6.70	7.00
Uganda	15.6	3.67	103	7.40	7.30
Middle Africa	60.2	3.03	137	—	6.24
Southern Africa	36.4	2.36	77	—	4.70
Botswana	1.1	3.71	67	4.90	7.10
Western Africa	165.1	3.19	111	—	6.85
Ghana	12.8	3.15	90	6.41	6.39
Nigeria	92.0	3.30	135	6.01	6.90
Senegal	6.4	2.78	87	6.60	6.50
Togo	3.0	3.07	94	6.94	6.58
Latin America	404.3	2.06	54	—	3.55
Asia	2835.2	1.87	72	—	3.48

NOTE: DHS stands for Demographic and Health Surveys; UN for the United Nations.

[a]Based on the United Nations' medium-variant population projection.

SOURCES: Total fertility rate, DHS, mid- to late-1980s—Institute for Resource Development (various years); other data—United Nations (1991).

1993), although fertility remains high by international standards. (United Nations estimates of the total fertility rates—the number of children per woman—are also shown in Table 2-5 for the purpose of international comparisons.) Some analysts have suggested that declines may have begun elsewhere, for example, in parts of Nigeria (Caldwell et al., 1992) and in Senegal (Cohen, 1993).

Although high by international standards, fertility is not as high as it might be. Nonsusceptibility to conception in the postpartum period continues to be a considerable inhibitor of fertility in Africa (Jolly and Gribble, 1993). Through breastfeeding and postpartum abstinence, many women are able to space the births of their children, so that the health of the children is enhanced.

Use of contraception is important at the national level in only three countries, Botswana, Kenya, and Zimbabwe. Among married women aged 15-49, 33, 27, and 43 percent, respectively, were using contraception in the late 1980s (Institute for Resource Development, 1991). Time spent out of marital unions has a greater fertility-reduction effect than contraception in the other African countries for which DHS data are available (Jolly and Gribble, 1993). There is evidence of some increase in the age at first marriage in Africa (van de Walle, 1993), but given the challenges of dating the beginnings of marital unions in Africa and problems of comparability of data sets, changes are difficult to quantify.

As mentioned earlier, in all of the seven countries studied here, Demographic and Health Surveys were conducted in the 1986-1990 period. Women aged 15-49 were asked about their marital histories, their past births, and whether their children had survived, as well as about their own socioeconomic characteristics. (Additional information about the surveys is presented in Appendix B.) These data can be used to locate in time vital events for each woman and child and allow us to link the vital events to changes in economic factors at the aggregate level. Before discussing our methodology in Chapter 4, however, we present our conceptual framework for making these connections and review other studies, primarily of a historical nature, that have attempted to assess the effects of changes in economic variables over time on demographic outcomes.

3

Conceptual Framework
and Hypotheses

This chapter addresses three questions that arise in constructing a framework for analyzing the relationship between economic indicators and demographic rates in a particular setting. First, what are the dominant sources of economic fluctuations within a region? Second, how do these fluctuations affect the types and levels of resources available to households? Third, how do changes in resources available to individuals and households affect demographic choices and outcomes? This chapter also examines the relations of economic shocks and demographic outcomes in preindustrial Europe and in other places in modern times, and briefly explores the relevance of those results for Africa.

TYPES OF FLUCTUATIONS

The vast array of sources of economic variation can be divided into three principal categories. The first category, which is especially relevant in simple agricultural economies, consists of variation in the local environment. As a result of fluctuations in temperature or rainfall, agricultural output will vary from year to year. This type of variation has figured heavily in the discussion of the relationship between economic variation and demographic rates in historical settings; analysis of this relationship has a long history (see Galloway, 1988, for a review of the literature, as well as his own analysis). Variations in agricultural conditions have also been identified as a significant factor underlying demographic behavior in developing countries (Caldwell, 1986; Rosenzweig, 1988; on the effect of famine, see Caldwell and Caldwell, 1987).

The second source of fluctuation is domestic political change, including changes in policy as well as political upheaval. The former may influence the availability of resources in two ways: by their effect on capital formation and economic growth; and by the way direct and indirect taxation and the provision of government services alter the distribution of resources. Domestic political factors may have played a relatively minor role in economic variation in the Europe of the past, but they have contributed substantially to economic changes in sub-Saharan Africa (see Chapter 2).

The third source of variation, fluctuations in the world economy, also has had more effect in contemporary developing countries than in historical populations. The prices of exported and imported goods, the availability of foreign aid, and the availability of credit all have played important roles in determining economic fluctuations in sub-Saharan Africa (see Chapter 2).

EFFECTS OF FLUCTUATIONS ON HOUSEHOLD RESOURCES

To assess the effect of a given type of shock on the resources available to households requires knowledge of the structure of the economic, political, and social systems in a particular region. Consider, for example, the effect of a widespread crop failure. In the absence of any form of storage or trade, the failure of the harvest in a particular region implies a similar reduction in the average resource availability in that region. When there is storage or trade, however, this relationship is weakened: Availability of food will fluctuate less than dictated by the crop in a particular year because in periods of shortage there will be an ability to draw down on existing stocks of grain or to import grain from other regions.

The possibilities for trade also influence the way fluctuations alter the distribution of resources within a country. In a country with both agriculture and manufacturing sectors, a negative agricultural shock not only reduces average resource availability but also affects the distribution of resources between the two sectors. The direction of the effect depends on how the price of the agricultural good, expressed in terms of the manufactured good, responds to the shock. Although each agricultural household produces less, it may receive a greater amount of manufactured good for each unit of the agricultural good it does produce. However, if there is trade with other regions at a fixed rate of exchange between the agricultural and manufactured good, the second effect will be absent and only agricultural households will have fewer resources.

This example illustrates another point about the distribution of resources: Shocks felt by one sector generally influence other sectors. Thus, a rise in international prices in one sector of the economy, say petroleum, can translate into increased purchasing power for households whose members work in that sector and thus into increased demand for both domestic and imported goods. Increased demand for domestic goods that are not easily traded, such as construction services, will translate into higher prices or growth in those sectors (or both), and thus will benefit households in those sectors and further stimulate economic activity. Households in sectors not benefiting either directly or indirectly from the favorable price movement may face an erosion of their purchasing power as the prices of these nontraded goods rise. A precise description of the magnitude and direction of these spillover effects is beyond the scope of this report, but the implication that shocks are not likely to be confined to one sector of the economy is of central importance.

Government policy also influences distributional effects. As Chapter 2 notes, when governments attempt to insulate domestic producers and consumers from international fluctuations by controlling producer prices of exported commodities, government revenues will vary as world prices fluctuate. And they will vary if import duties are an important source of government revenue and fluctuations in world prices affect domestic demand for these imported goods. The effect of this variation in government revenue on the domestic economy depends on the distribution of these resources. If revenues are channeled directly into particular sectors of the economy then these sectors are the primary beneficiaries of favorable price movements even if they are not the ones actually producing or consuming the traded commodity.

Finally, distributional effects vary with the pervasiveness and the persistence of the shock and with the ability of individuals to transfer resources across space and time. A single crop failure in a particular year for an individual farmer has only a limited effect on his resources in that year if he can transfer resources from another place or another time through the formal sector (say, bank loans or government-sponsored crop insurance) or the informal sector (say, loans or transfers from family or friends).

The medium-term effects of economic shocks on household resources depend on the ability of individuals to shift away from activities that may have become less profitable toward more profitable ones. For example, facing a sustained decline in the price for his primary crop, a farmer may shift to other crops, attempt to sell the crop on the black market (if the decline is as a result of government policy), or give up farming altogether. The availability of alternative activities is sensitive to many factors: the types of crops being grown (for example, crops with a long growing cycle admit less flexibility than those grown in a single year); the diversity of the economy (whether, say, jobs are available in manufacturing); and aspects of government policy. Thus, the medium-run effects of shocks on household resources may vary substantially from country to country.

Beyond affecting the overall level of resources available to particular households, economic fluctuations affect the types of resources available largely through their effect on the relative prices of different goods that the household consumes or uses. Of particular importance for our study are changes in the costs of raising children, including both direct and opportunity costs. These costs may change as a result of market response, for example, a rise in the price of food following a crop shortage; however, in countries with a strong government sector, changes in health, education, and family planning services provided by the government may also affect such costs. Changes in government expenditures may stem from changes in government priorities or in overall revenues, both of which may, in turn, stem from changes in domestic or international conditions.

EFFECTS OF CHANGES IN HOUSEHOLD RESOURCES ON DEMOGRAPHIC EVENTS

The theoretical basis for the literature examining the relationship between aggregate economic indicators and demographic rates is the Malthusian argument that increases in real wages foster increases in marriage or fertility (or both) and decreases in mortality. In the case of mortality, this relationship is straightforward. In both cross-national and individual-level analyses higher levels of wealth are associated with lower levels of mortality, particularly at low levels of income (Preston, 1980). Because it worsens the environment or occupational safety, rapid economic growth may adversely affect the mortality of particular groups within a country; but these effects are likely to be dominated by the improvements in nutrition and health care associated with income growth. Although there is general agreement about the relationship between income and mortality in both the short and the long term, there remains substantial debate about the mechanisms responsible for this relationship. In particular, the relative importance of starvation, synergy between poor nutrition and infection, and exposure to disease as a result of migration or other behaviors, including, for example, weaning, has not been established.

Short-run variations in mortality, the focus of this study, and long-run variations do not necessarily respond to the same aspects of resource availability. For example, Mata (1985, 1987) emphasizes the roles of infection control and "maternal technologies" in the decline of child mortality in Costa Rica. In the short run, economic conditions may not affect control of infection, say, through vector control or water sanitation programs, but long-run neglect of such programs is likely to have substantial effects on infection and on child mortality. Similarly, maternal technologies, which are acquired behaviors favorable to child survival and through which maternal education may exert much of its effect, may be resistant to short-term economic changes.

Even more important is distinguishing short- and long-run economic

effects on fertility and marriage because of the complexity of the relationship that links economic change and these events in the long run. There is
not a clear consensus about the mechanisms underlying the long-run relationship between economic change and fertility, but the causes of short-term
variation in marriage and fertility rates are well understood. The marriage
rate may be positively correlated with resource availability either because
of the explicit costs associated with the process of marriage (e.g., payment
of bridewealth) or because of a perceived need for a certain level of financial security before marriage. For fertility, during periods of scarcity the
dominant factors are likely to be conscious attempts to limit fertility in
contracepting populations, delayed weaning, and the effects of migration
and other forms of adaptation. The role of nutritional subfecundity has
received substantial attention, but, except during periods of extreme scarcity, the evidence for such an effect is weak (Menken et al., 1981). Although economic theory focusing on the time-cost of children suggests a
possible negative relationship between wages and fertility in the short-run
(Butz and Ward, 1979), the evidence is not conclusive (Murphy, 1992).

In the cases of both mortality and fertility, a distinction should be made
between the immediate and cumulative effects of an economic shock. Models that incorporate heterogeneity in the risk of death suggest that periods of
higher than average mortality will be followed by periods of lower than
average mortality if the initial high mortality leads to a disproportionate
number of deaths among the frailest members of the population. However,
if the cause of the initial high mortality also results in the debilitation of a
large proportion of the population, then higher than average mortality may
persist into the later period. In the former case, the cumulative effect of a
given shock would be smaller than suggested by the short-run effect, whereas
in the latter it would exceed the immediate effect (Vaupel et al., 1988). The
heterogeneity argument potentially applies in the context of marriage and
fertility. The case of fertility is complicated, however, by the interval of
gestation and by the connection that runs from the reduction in breastfeeding
following a period of low fertility directly to a decrease in lactational amenorrhea
and thence to an increase in fertility when effective contraception is not
practiced. Thus in societies with low levels of contraceptive use and prolonged breastfeeding the cumulative effect of a given reduction in fertility
can be considerably smaller than the immediate effect.

Moreover, a given variation in resource availability may have different
effects on demographic behavior and processes as economic development
proceeds. For example, widespread implementation in the 1980s of primary
health care strategies might be expected to have weakened the link between
economic conditions and child mortality, whereas the increased availability
of modern contraceptive methods might have strengthened the link between
economic conditions and fertility. The improvement in average health that

comes from long-run increases in economic resources may also reduce the chance that even sizable economic reversals will result in an increased risk of death. And if contraceptives are available and culturally acceptable, economic recession may not mean a reduction in the marriage rate, because of the possibility of marriage without the expectation of rapid childbearing.

SHORT-TERM VARIATION IN PREINDUSTRIAL EUROPE

Much of the literature on the relation of variation in macroeconomic conditions and vital rates focuses on the effects of grain prices in preindustrial Europe (Lee, 1981; Galloway, 1988). The usual justification for this approach is that given the rigidity of nominal wages in this setting, the price of basic foodstuffs is a good measure of variation in real wages and therefore of resource availability. This justification does not apply directly to households that are net producers of a commodity (a nonnegligible fraction of preindustrial populations). Nevertheless, at least in an economy with limited access to trade and storage, grain prices reflect grain production and, therefore for net producers as well, they can be negatively correlated with household resource availability.

Results from these analyses have yielded quite consistent results. Births are negatively related to prices; the largest effect comes after one year. Marriages are also negatively related to real prices, but here the largest effect occurs in the same year. Post-infant mortality is positively associated with real prices; again, the largest effect comes with a one-year lag, though substantial effects appear both in the current year and with a two-year lag. A particularly useful paper by Galloway (1988) uses a consistent methodology to evaluate these effects in a variety of populations. There is considerable variation across populations in the elasticities (the percentage change in one variable as a result of a 1 percent change in another variable), but typically elasticities are on the order of 0.1. Thus a 10 percent increase in grain prices leads to an decrease of approximately 1 percent in fertility and marriage and to a 1 percent increase in mortality. Finally, Galloway detects a weakening of the observed relationship between prices and mortality in countries that are more developed economically.

MEASURING SHORT-TERM VARIATION
IN OTHER POPULATIONS

The links between economic conditions and mortality levels in developed countries in the twentieth century have been subject to more controversy. In a series of articles focusing primarily on postwar Britain, Brenner (1973, 1983, 1987) identifies significant short- and medium-term associations between economic instability and a range of mortality outcomes that includes neonatal, postneonatal, child, and adult mortality specific by cause, particularly ischemic heart disease. However, Brenner's analyses have been criticized on the grounds of an inappropriate lag structure (McAvinchey and Wagstaff, 1987).

Without doubt fertility responded to the Great Depression and has continued since to be affected by economic conditions (Easterlin, 1965). The lows in fertility experienced in the 1930s in the now-developed countries were clearly due in part to the economic conditions of the time.

The experience of the Dutch Hunger Winter (1944-1945) is also relevant. After a blockade was imposed on a part of the Dutch population, nutritional status deteriorated, and reductions in fertility and increases in mortality were also observed (Stein et al., 1975). The relatively obvious beginning and end of the period of scarcity made it possible to attribute at least some of the reduction in fertility to an increase in fetal wastage.

Evidence of economic-demographic relationships in developing countries is much weaker, in part because the statistical infrastructure is much less well developed. Direct evidence of the effects of the Great Depression on demographic conditions in the developing world is scarce, but indirect evidence suggest linkages. Hill (1991) analyzes age distributions from 34 developing countries with at least three censuses after World War II, and detects a strong effect of the 1930s in that the cohorts surviving from the period are smaller than those surviving from the immediately preceding or following decades. In the absence of large migratory flows, small cohorts may result from a reduction in the number of births or an increase in mortality risks in childhood. The indirect analysis does not pinpoint the responsible factor, although evidence from a small number of countries with good data suggests that both contributed.

In addition, there are some clear-cut individual cases of demographic responses to economic and social changes. It is now well documented that the economic crisis and famine in China at around the time of the Great Leap Forward had far-reaching effects on both fertility and mortality (Ashton et al., 1984; Coale, 1984). Fertility fell to about half its precrisis level in the period 1958-1961, and then rebounded for two years to levels not previously recorded in China. Child mortality soared: The infant mortality rate in 1958 was more than double its precrisis level, but the rate fell to below the earlier level almost as soon as the crisis ended. Mortality risks for the elderly also rose steeply during the three-year crisis; working-age adults were the least affected. The demographic responses in China were approximately those that would have been expected, given the changes observed in real prices, on the basis of preindustrial European experience (Lee, 1990).

The 1974 famine in Bangladesh, which was precipitated by the more than doubling of rice prices over two months, has also received substantial attention. Ravallion (1987) showed that the increase in mortality kept close

pace with the increase in the price of rice; the short- and long-run elasticities, estimated at the mean price of rice were 0.14 and 0.23, respectively.
By fitting a model that incorporated quadratic terms Ravallion also found
evidence of nonlinear effects. At one standard deviation above the mean
price, the short- and long-run elasticities were 0.50 and 0.81, respectively.
He also noted that 12 percent of the monthly variation in mortality over the
four years surrounding the famine could be explained using the price data.
Razzaque and his colleagues (1990) found that the effects of the famine on
mortality were not uniform: Better-off households experienced little effect.

Since the publication of the UNICEF volumes *The Impact of World
Recession on Children* (Jolly and Cornia, 1984) and *Adjustment with a Human Face* (Cornia et al., 1987), attempts have been made to examine the
empirical basis for the argument that economic downturns in general and
adjustment policies in particular have been associated with increases in
infant and child mortality in recent decades. No evidence of any systematic
change in the pace of child mortality decline in the developing world in the
early 1980s emerged from a study by Hill and Pebley (1989); but Palloni
and Tienda (1991) found that gains in infant survival in Chile and Costa
Rica for the 1980s were below what would have been expected on the basis
of trends.

Analyses similar in methodology to those of historical European populations have been carried out using vital registration data (see, for example,
Taucher, 1989; Bravo, 1992; Hill and Palloni, 1992). In general, these analyses
have confirmed that economic-demographic relationships similar to those
operating in preindustrial Europe applied in the countries studied, though
the effects on mortality were muted. However, these studies were limited to
countries with good vital statistics systems, which were all in Latin America.
For example, Hill and Palloni (1992) applied a methodology similar to that
used by Lee (1981) and Galloway (1988) to vital registration data for selected countries of Latin America, and found a negative relationship between economic change and change in infant mortality that is significant if
all country observations are pooled in a single sample; they also found a
positive relationship between economic conditions and both marriages and
births, very much in line with findings from preindustrial Europe in both
direction and magnitude.

Less work has been done on Africa, largely because almost all sub-
Saharan African countries lack the vital registration system that is the natural data base for time-series analysis. Some attempts have been made to
examine the consequences for child mortality of economic recession in sub-
Saharan Africa using retrospective data from Living Standards Measurement Surveys as a source of time-series data (see, for example, Diop (1990)
and Saadah (1991)); but the sample sizes are small, and the studies found
few results that were both significant and plausible.

THE RELEVANCE FOR AFRICA OF
RESULTS FROM OTHER STUDIES

Given the preponderance of evidence supporting a relationship between economic and demographic variation, some relationships are likely to emerge for sub-Saharan Africa. Nonetheless, this region and others that have been studied differ in important ways.

The first difference has to do with the origin of the economic variation. Although the shocks in agricultural output that dominated fluctuations in real wages in preindustrial Europe are likely to be significant in the agricultural regions of Africa, the increase in the importance of international trade and capital flows, coupled with the substantial role of the public sector, has diminished the relative importance of this type of shock. These other types of fluctuations may be as large as, or larger than, those resulting from environmental conditions, but they introduce additional complications.

First, no single, easily collected measure adequately reflects the extent of variation for Africa the way that grain prices do for preindustrial Europe. Although aggregate measures of economic activity such as real gross national product could, in principle, meet this need, their accuracy as measures of short-term variation in economic conditions in countries with large informal or subsistence sectors is suspect. Direct measures of external shocks such as those in world prices or terms of trade are more easily measured, but they capture only one component of the variation in economic conditions, and so there arises a problem of omitted-variable bias in any analysis of the relationship between them and demographic rates. Finally, the periodicity of politically and internationally driven shocks is likely to be substantially longer than that of shocks driven by weather; thus identifying the effect of economic shocks over relatively short time horizons becomes more difficult.

Besides the differences in the origin of economic shocks, their effects on household resource availability in Africa today are also likely to differ from those in preindustrial Europe. Differences in the ability to transfer resources across time and space, the importance of international trade and capital flows, the opportunity for undertaking new activities in response to changing conditions, and the role played by the government sector all affect both the magnitude and the distribution of the effect of a given shock on household resource availability. It is difficult to assess the implications of this variegated pattern for an analysis of the demographic effects of economic fluctuations because many effects are offsetting. For example, the spread of government health and family planning services may either dampen some of the effects of economic shocks or amplify them, depending on how expenditures in these areas are determined. An increase in trade decreases the effect of domestic environmental shocks on resource availability but increases exposure to fluctuations in international conditions.

Sub-Saharan Africa and preindustrial Europe seem to be most comparable in the relationship between resource availability and demographic behaviors. Although, as argued above, widespread availability of primary health care and contraceptives could alter the relationship between fluctuations in household resources and demographic events, the relative scarcity of these services in sub-Saharan Africa until very recently limits the potential importance of their effects. Although direct comparisons are difficult, by some measures sub-Saharan Africa and preindustrial Europe do not differ substantially in overall levels of wealth, at least in comparison to the currently developed countries (Cratts, 1983). However, it is possible that fertility and marriage in sub-Saharan Africa represent quite different social phenomena than they did in preindustrial Europe. Some have argued, for example, that the sustained high levels of fertility in Africa may be attributed in part to important cultural supports that are unique to that region (see Caldwell, 1987). Such social phenomena as coresidence of extended family members and the fostering of small children may reduce the incentives to limit childbearing during periods of adversity.

4

Methodology

Among the choices faced in designing the analysis of child mortality, marriage, and first and second births were the following:

- what types of models to fit—time patterns of simple counts of events, logistic regressions of event probabilities, or Poisson regressions of event rates;
- how to identify time patterns of change, enter economic factors into the models, and control for secular changes that might affect the demographic outcomes; and
- whether or not to control for individual characteristics of women and children.

Each of these topics is addressed below. This chapter also describes the analyses of marriage and fertility and of mortality and discusses hypothesis testing and interpretation of results.

TYPES OF MODELS

To identify the short-run effects of economic variation on demographic outcomes, we would ideally use long time series of both economic and demographic data and attempt to ascertain similarities in patterns of change. We have indeed been able to assemble time series of economic information at the national level for our seven study countries (see Appendix A), but in most developing countries, and in sub-Saharan Africa in particular, reliable time series are not available on marriages, births, or deaths. Vital registration systems that record such demographic events are nonexistent or operate only partially, and there have not been periodic surveys or censuses of sufficiently good quality and with appropriate questions for us to piece together time series.

Fortunately, the Demographic and Health Surveys (DHS) conducted in the late 1980s in the countries that we have chosen for study provide sufficient individual-level information so that we can locate in time a woman's first marriage, her children's births, and her children's deaths.[1] In these surveys, women aged 15-49 were asked about their dates of entry into first marital union, the dates of the births of their children, the ages at death of any children who had died, and their own socioeconomic characteristics, such as education. Such survey data are not ideal for our purposes. For one thing, only a limited number of demographic outcomes can be studied; for example, no information is available on adult mortality. Also, the data are affected by the usual problems of recall error associated with retrospective data. Moreover, as time passes, the composition of women and children in the reconstructed time series changes, so we must use a multivariate approach that takes into consideration the exposure of the woman or child to the risk of the demographic outcome in each calendar period. Such a multivariate approach also has the advantage of providing information on the precision of our estimates of variation in the demographic variables.

The basic approach we use for all four of the demographic outcomes is to estimate life tables with regressors. These regressors include the economic variables of concern, as well as controls for sample composition, which will be discussed later. For marriage, first birth, and second birth, we analyze the probabilities of events occurring by fitting a discrete-time hazard model that is based on logistic regression. For child mortality, we analyze the rates at which events occur by using Poisson regression. Both procedures applied to a particular outcome should yield the same substantive results, and the choice between them is essentially one of the preference of the researcher (Trussell and Guinnane, 1993).

For example, in the case of our analysis of marriage, we use the survey information to ascertain the calendar years in which an individual woman was at risk of being married for the first time[2] and whether or not she

---

[1] See Appendix B for information about the dates and sample sizes of the surveys, as well as a discussion of data quality.

[2] It is assumed that exposure to the risk of being married or giving birth the first time for a given calendar period begins at age 10 or the beginning of the current period, whichever is later; exposure to the risk of having a second birth for a given period begins at the birth of the first child or the beginning of the current period, whichever is later; and exposure of a child to the risk of dying in a given period begins at its birth or the beginning of the current period, whichever is later.

became married in that year.[3]   Each unit of exposure for each woman, measured in years, is treated as a separate and independent observation, and we use a discrete-time hazard model to estimate the effects of macroeconomic factors on marriage, as we discuss in the next section.

The data compilation is essentially the same for the analysis of first and second births; but for the analysis of child mortality, we use month as the unit of analysis and characterize children by their ages in months because risks of mortality change considerably from month to month in the first year of life.   Using months to measure both calendar time and the length of exposure to the risk of dying in the Poisson regression models of child mortality that we fit allows us to locate more accurately both events and exposure to the risk of dying in calendar years during which economic conditions may have been quite different.

ECONOMIC VARIABLES AND SECULAR TRENDS

In both the discrete-time hazard and the Poisson models, two approaches are used to identify the time patterns of fluctuations in the rates of demographic events and to estimate relationships between these events and fluctuations in macroeconomic indicators: (1) Time effects are estimated using dummy variables for each calendar year net of a linear trend, and (2) economic indicators are entered directly into the regressions that also include a trend term.

We are concerned about controlling for the trend because we do not want to confuse short-term variations in the pattern of events or short-term effects of economic conditions on these events with long-term changes in society and the economy that do not directly enter into our models. We use only a linear trend rather than a higher-order configuration because we have no strong expectation about the order and because, given the complexity of our models, introducing a higher-order term would further limit our already limited degrees of freedom.

The same economic variables are used for analysis of marriages, births, and child deaths (see Table 4-1 for a list).   The basic model relates the deviation from trend in year t of a demographic variable to the value of an economic variable in year t (no lag), the previous year $t - 1$ (lag one), and the year before that $t - 2$ (lag two).   This model is estimated separately for each demographic variable, each economic variable, each country, and, for as many countries as possible, urban and rural populations.   We use logarithms of the economic variables because this practice, common in econom-

---

[3] There is some ambiguity about the precise timing of union formation in Africa.   See van de Walle (1993) for a discussion.

TABLE 4-1   Economic Variables Used in the Marriage, Fertility, and
Mortality Analyses for Seven Sub-Saharan African Countries

Economic Variable	Country						
	Botswana	Ghana	Kenya	Nigeria	Senegal	Togo	Uganda
Real GDP per capita (GDP)	X	X	X	X	X	X	X
Export quantum index (EXQ)		X	X	X	X	X	X
Terms of trade (TT)		X	X	X	X	X	X
Cocoa output (QCOC)		X					
Rainfall (RAIN)					X		
Real world price							
Cocoa (WPCOC)		X		X		X	
Coffee (WPCOF)			X			X	X
Cotton (WPCOT)							X
Groundnuts (WPGN)					X		
Petroleum (WPOIL)				X			
Phosphates (WPPH)					X	X	
Tea (WPTEA)			X				
Real producer price							
Cocoa (PPCOC)		X		X		X	
Coffee (PPCOF)			X			X	
Groundnuts (PPGN)					X		

NOTE: Definitions of variables and sources of data are given in Appendix A.

ics, typically yields better fits and because the coefficients on the economic variables can be interpreted as elasticities, given the logarithmic nature of our dependent variables. We discuss this matter in a later section of this chapter.

We use lagged values of the economic variables for the two previous years, as well as the current value, because the historical literature and common sense suggest that changes in the macroeconomy may not be perceived or experienced at the micro level for some time (see Chapter 3). Moreover, there may be some lag associated with a biological or behavioral response to a given economic shock; for example, delays to conception and a gestation period of nine months imply that effects on fertility will almost inevitably be lagged. Including a lag structure further reduces the degrees of freedom in the models, so we decided to go back only two years, rather than five, say, and to make no effort to test for the symmetry of effects, that is, whether upturns and downturns in the economy had effects of the same magnitude and opposite sign.

Only one economic variable (and its lagged values) is entered into each model, rather than including several economic indicators at once and allowing them to compete. The primary reason is that the economic indicators are imperfectly measured and in many cases highly correlated, so any attempt to apportion effects among them would be unproductive. More basically, our null hypothesis is that there are no effects, so if we find any effects, we have learned something.

For some of the economic variables, data were not available for the most recent years, and the analysis had to be truncated. For the analysis of marriages and births, data for the 25 years preceding the country's DHS were used, where possible. For the mortality analysis, the periods covered were from 1970 to the year before the survey in each country, where possible.[4] In the tables in Chapter 5 that present the results, specific time periods are given for each part of the analysis and each economic variable.

CONTROL VARIABLES

A final general question in designing the analysis plan was whether to control for characteristics of the women—for example, their age, residence (urban or rural), education—and for characteristics of the children—for example, their age, birth order, the length of previous birth interval.

We have controlled for factors that affect sample composition, that is, age of women in the marriage and fertility analyses. Because we are concerned with economic effects on the probabilities of "surviving" to specific ages or durations, we have also included variables related to duration of exposure to the risk of the demographic event: for second births, the interval since first birth, and for child mortality, the age of the child. (For marriages and first births, the age of the woman serves this purpose also.) Given our interest in economic effects, some of which may be felt more strongly in urban or rural areas, we have also fit models separately for urban and rural samples for both types of analysis, where possible, as discussed later.

In the results presented in the tables in Chapter 5, we have not con-

---

[4]For Kenya, the survey fieldwork began in December 1988. Because the exposure period for the marriage and birth analysis is years, the years considered are 1963 to 1987. For the mortality analysis, which uses exposure in terms of months, the data for 1988 were also used.

trolled for any other factors. We experimented with other controls that are frequently included in models of the demographic outcomes considered here, but their inclusion had only marginal effects on the results about time patterns or economic effects. Any dramatic differences in results yielded by the inclusion of these controls are mentioned in the discussion in Chapter 5. Otherwise, for the sake of parsimony, the results are not presented.

The controls with which we experimented fall into two basic categories: those that change slowly over time and those that may change rapidly. In the category of controls that change slowly over time is one that may affect the trend in all the demographic outcomes: the education of the woman or mother. Given the increase in educational attainment of women over time in all of the study countries, women with exposure to risk of events in the early years of the analysis would be disproportionately less educated. Thus, the education variable is a means of controlling for secular changes in the demographic behaviors, beyond the inclusion of a trend variable in our analyses.

In the category of controls that may vary rapidly over time are several we tried in the mortality analysis. One is the survival of the previous child born to the mother of the child being considered; it may help remove interhousehold heterogencity and thus make more plausible our assumption of the independence of mortality of children of the same mother. Another is the length of the previous birth interval, which controls for the effects of fertility on child mortality. Suppose, for example, that economic variables affect mortality indirectly (by influencing the duration of the previous birth interval) as well as directly (by changing resource availability). Then an analysis of the effects of economic variables on mortality that did not control for fertility might show a relationship but would provide no insight into the mechanism underlying it. An analysis controlling for the length of the previous birth interval could in principle allow one to distinguish the direct and indirect effects; however, the results could be misleading if important determinants of both birth spacing and mortality, such as maternal health, say, are unobservable to the researcher. Finally, there are other controls that may be endogenous to the models (e.g., the birth order of the child) or controls that may be determined by some unobservable factors that also influence child mortality, so that the resulting coefficients may be misleading. A full list of the controls included for experimental purposes for each country in the mortality analysis is provided in a later section.

METHODOLOGY FOR ANALYSIS OF MARRIAGE AND BIRTHS

The procedures used for the analyses of marriage, first births, and second births are essentially the same with differences only in the definition of the dependent variable. The basic model estimates the log odds of an event occurring as follows:

$$\ln \frac{q_{it}}{1-q_{it}} = \sum_{a=1}^{6} \beta_a \delta_{iat} + \tau' X_i + \beta_t + \gamma t,$$

where in the case of marriage q_{it} is the probability that individual i becomes married in year t given that she is unmarried at the start of year t; δ_{iat} is 1 if individual i is age a on June 30 of year t and 0 otherwise; X_i is a vector of characteristics for individual i; β_a represents age effects with six categories of age;[5] τ is a vector of coefficients associated with X_i; β_t represents the effects of specific calendar years; and γ is the effect of the trend t.

In the second stage of the analysis, the effects of economic indicators for each year and the two previous years are substituted for the effects of specific calendar years.   The next to the last term in the above equation becomes

$$\sum_{L=0}^{2} \pi_L \ln Z_{t-L}$$

where $\ln Z_{t-L}$ is the logarithm of the value of the economic variable in year t minus the lag L, which ranges from 0 to 2 years, and π_L is the effect of the economic variable at lag L.

Note that this model, which is known as a discrete-time hazard model (see Allison, 1982, and Foster et al., 1986), assumes that variation in first marriage rates is driven primarily by period factors; indeed, the time dummies are assumed to have the same effects on the log odds of marriage at each age in a given period. This assumption seems reasonable given the focus on the effects of macroeconomic indicators that are themselves period measures. Although cohort factors may play some role in determining the age pattern of marriage, they are unlikely to dominate year-to-year fluctuations in marriage rates.[6]

---

[5]In the case of the marriage analysis, a piecewise-linear spline (Neter and Wasserman (1974) develop and review this technique) based on the following six age groups is used: 10-14, 14-16, 16-18, 18-22, 22-26, and 26-30 years. For first births, a spline with four age groups, 10-18, 18-22, 22-26, and 26-30 years, is used. For the analysis of second births, the same age groups plus birth-interval dummy variables (1, 2, 3, and 4 plus years) are used. The birth-interval dummies refer to completed years since last birth on June 30 of the corresponding calendar year. Ages refer to age on June 30 of the corresponding year.

[6]Some researchers would argue that another important assumption of this model is that the individual years of observation for each woman, our units of analysis, are assumed to be independent. Violation of this assumption, which is likely but about which nothing can be done, may result in biased estimates of parameters and standard errors (see Heckman and Walker (1990) for a discussion). Other researchers, however, disagree (see Trussell and Guinnane, 1993).

This model is estimated using a weighted logistic regression in which, for marriage and first and second births, a piecewise-linear age curve is assumed (see footnote 5). In the more usual approach the coefficient on the corresponding dummy variable for an age group can be interpreted as the level of log odds of marriage at the corresponding ages. In contrast, when piecewise-linear variables are used each coefficient can be interpreted as the slope of the log odds of the marriage hazard in that duration. The advantage of this approach over the usual one is that, rather than assuming a constant hazard in each age category, the hazard is allowed to increase (or decrease) linearly.

For the marriage and fertility analysis, we included in some of our models only one other variable not specific to age, duration, or period—a variable indicating whether or not the woman had any education. We chose this variable because it was the only one available from DHS that could reasonably be assumed to have been resolved before the time of marriage and the first two births. Information was available on other socioeconomic characteristics of the women at the time of the survey, but there was little guarantee that it was relevant for past periods. The results from models including education as a control are reported only when they are substantially different from those models without it.

As mentioned earlier, where possible, the analysis was done separately for urban and rural women, given our interest in the differential effects of economic factors in these areas. Because of the possibility of migration between age 10, when we assume exposure to the risks of marriage and first birth begin, and the times of marriage or first or second birth and because migration histories were not collected as part of the DHS, we use the woman's residence at age 12 to split the total sample into urban and rural samples of women. Clearly, this variable is imperfect as a proxy for the woman's residence at the times of marriage and the first two births, but it was the best information at hand. Unfortunately, even this information was not available for Botswana and Uganda.

For the analysis of fertility we consider only first and second births because the numbers of births decline rapidly as birth order increases, and because of the severe conditionality constraints applied to higher-order births (for example, only a woman who has already had exactly two births can have a third). This constraint on sample size is especially severe for the early years of our analysis, the early 1960s, when the oldest DHS respondents, aged 45-49 at the time of the surveys, would have been only in their early twenties. We analyze first and second births separately because we expect that the effects of socioeconomic factors may differ for these essentially different demographic phenomena.

METHODOLOGY FOR ANALYSIS OF CHILD MORTALITY

The procedure used for analyzing child mortality, Poisson regression, is slightly different from that used for marriage and fertility, although the broad steps of the analysis are the same. In the first step, dummy variables representing calendar years and a variable for the linear trend are included in the model; in the second step, the calendar-year variables are replaced by the corresponding values of one of the economic indicators, plus the value of that indicator for the previous two years, lags one and two.

Poisson regression is essentially a methodology for the multivariate analysis of counts of occurrences, in this case, of child deaths. The method assumes some underlying risk or hazard of the event occurring in some category of duration of exposure, in this case an age group of children. In our model, the natural logarithm of the hazard, h_{ia}, for observation i of age group a is assumed to be given by an additive expression including the base hazard for the age group, h_a, and the effects of a series of other variables X that are assumed to influence the hazard:

$$\ln(h_{ia}) = h_a + \tau'X_i \, .$$

Note that in our model the effects of the variables X are assumed not to vary with age.

The expected number of events or deaths, D'_{ia}, observed for individuals with a particular set of characteristics in duration-of-exposure category a, will be the hazard multiplied by the exposure time of such individuals in the exposure category, E_{ia}. Thus for individuals with characteristics i and age a,

$$D'_{ia} = E_{ia} \cdot h_{ia}$$

or

$$D'_{ia} = E_{ia} \cdot e^{h_a + \tau'X_i}$$

or

$$D'_{ia} = e^{\ln(E_{ia}) + h_a + \tau'X_i} \, .$$

Then taking logarithms and subtracting the first term on the right from both sides yields:

$$\ln(D'_{ia}) - \ln(E_{ia}) = h_a + \tau'X_i \, .$$

The logarithm of the exposure term E_{ia} is commonly referred to as the "offset," which standardizes cell counts for varying exposure times.

In our application, we are interested primarily in variations over time. Thus the variable of interest is calendar time; other variables are included in the model to allow for variations in other factors that might conceal or confound the underlying relationships with time. Thus the model can be summarized as

$$\ln(D'_{iat}) - \ln(E_{iat}) = h_a + \tau'X_i + \beta_t + \gamma t$$

for individuals of control characteristics i and age a in calendar year t, where t is continuous time to capture a constant rate of change. In a second step of the analysis, the effects of the calendar-year dummies, β_t, are replaced by the effects of the current and lagged values of one of the economic indicators, as indicated in the discussion of the analysis of marriage and fertility.

Just as in that analysis, we are not interested primarily in the coefficients on the vector of control variables X and do not report them. Note, however, that none of the coefficients in the model varies with a, the exposure category (age of child). Thus it is assumed that the effects of the independent variables do not vary, that is, that they have the same proportional effect on the hazard across all age categories.

The data are set up for Poisson analysis by counting events (deaths) and exposure time in each cell of a matrix defined by age a, time t, and a vector of control variables X. The Poisson model assumes that the hazard does not vary within exposure categories a, so we tried to adopt categories within which the mortality rate can be regarded as essentially constant. However, we also had to take into account typical data distortions, whereby a disproportionate number of deaths may be reported at age 12 months. The age at death of children in the DHS was supposed to be recorded in days for children who died before reaching the age of 1 month, in months for those children who died at ages from 1 month to 23 months, and in years for children dying after age 2 years. However, in several surveys, a substantial proportion of deaths were reported as having occurred at age 1 year, without the month being specified. In Botswana and Kenya for which the latter problem was minor, we used age categories 0 months, 1 to 3 months, 4 to 9 months, 10 to 15 months (to spread the 12-month reports over their likely range of true values), 16 to 23 months, 24 to 35 months, 36 to 47 months, and 48 to 59 months. In the remaining countries, in which substantial numbers of deaths were reported as occurring at age 1 year, we collapsed the fourth and fifth categories into a single category for 10 to 23 months.

As mentioned earlier, the reason that months instead of years are used to measure both deaths and exposure to the risk of death is that the risk of death in the early months and years of life changes dramatically. Risks of marriage and fertility change more slowly as exposure changes.

In our mortality models, we have assumed that the effects of the economic and other control variables are proportional across all age groups. To explore the potential importance of this constraint, we have fitted the mortality models separately for specific age groups to see whether the relationships with economic change differ by age group. They generally do not differ greatly, so only the few results by age that are significant and of interest are mentioned in Chapter 5.

As noted earlier, we experimented with including a number of control variables in the mortality analysis. The characteristics of the children and their mothers that were included were selected by fitting two preliminary models for each country. The first model included what we refer to as "physiological" variables, such as sex of the child, age of the mother (<20, 20-34, ≥35 years), interactions of birth order (1, 2-4, 5+) with survival of the previous child (for the last two categories of birth order), interactions of birth order with the length of the previous birth interval (<24, 24-47, ≥48 months; once again for the last two categories of birth order). These physiological variables typically have significant effects in analyses of infant and child mortality in developing countries (see, for example, Hobcraft et al., 1985).

The second preliminary model included variables from the first model that had significant effects plus individual-level socioeconomic variables, such as education (usually coded as no education versus some, but in the cases of Botswana and Kenya as no education, primary education, more than primary); ethnicity (Akan for Ghana (ultimately dropped), Luhya/Luo for Kenya, Adjaewe for Togo, Muganda for Uganda); religion (Christian or not); and in one case, Nigeria, region of the country (North). Once again, these variables were selected because of their general importance in earlier work on mortality and because preliminary inspection of the data indicated substantial variation in mortality by these categories. In the final preliminary model, as many of the significant variables as possible, given technical constraints, were included. Table 4-2 lists the variables for each country.

As in the analysis of marriage and first and second births, however, for the sake of parsimony, in Chapter 5 we present the results of the analysis without these control variables. Although the inclusion of some of the variables may be important for controlling the changing composition of the sample over time—for example, the education of mothers—the inclusion of others may mask some of the effects of changes in economic conditions. For example, economic decline could act to lengthen the intervals between births, a development that might be expected to result in declines in child mortality. However, as discussed earlier, whether to include the length of the previous birth interval in the mortality equation remains an open question.[7] As in the case of the marriage and fertility analysis, the results do

---

[7]The uncontrolled model does have the advantage of paralleling more closely the historical analyses of aggregate events.

TABLE 4-2 Individual-Level Variables Used in the Mortality Analysis for Seven Sub-Saharan African Countries

Variable	Botswana	Ghana	Kenya	Nigeria	Senegal	Togo	Uganda
Male	X	X					X
Young mother			X	X	X	X	
Old mother		X					
Birth order							
1	X	X	X	X	X	X	X
2-4 • short previous interval	X	X	X	X	X	X	X
5+ • short previous interval	X	X	X	X	X	X	X
2-4 • medium previous interval					X		X
5+ • medium previous interval					X	X	X
2-4 • previous child died	X	X	X	X	X	X	X
5+ • previous child died	X	X	X	X	X	X	X
No education	X	X	X	X	X		X
Primary education	X		X				
Rural		X		X	X	X	
Christian		X	X	X		X	
Ethnicity							
Luhya/Luo			X				
Adjaewe						X	
Muganda							X
Region				X^a			
Age (months)							
0	X	X	X	X	X	X	X
1-3	X	X	X	X	X	X	X
4-9	X	X	X	X	X	X	X
10-15	X		X				
10-23		X		X	X	X	X
16-23	X		X				
24-35	X	X	X	X	X	X	X
36-47	X	X	X	X	X	X	X
48-59	X	X	X	X	X	X	X

[a]North region.

not differ substantially between models with and without these control variables. The few cases in which they do are mentioned in Chapter 5.

Also, as in the analysis of marriage and fertility, in the mortality analysis we are interested in the differential effects of economic factors in urban and rural areas. Accordingly, where possible (Ghana, Nigeria, Senegal, and Togo), we fit models first for the total sample of children, then separately for children in urban areas and children in rural areas. The DHS did not collect migration histories from each mother. To assign a given child's experience to the appropriate category of residence, we had to compare the birthdate of the child with information on how many years the mother had lived in her current residence at the time of the survey. Thus, in the urban and rural samples, we include only children whose mother had not moved since their births and assigned her locale to the child. For Botswana, this calculation was not possible because the question about length of residence was not asked. Moreover, in Kenya and Uganda, given the relatively small number of urban dwellers, it was not possible to do the analysis separately for children in urban areas, and the rural children dominated the total sample.

HYPOTHESIS TESTING AND INTERPRETATION OF RESULTS

For each of the demographic outcomes—marriage, first and second births, and child mortality—we tested for the following in the first stage of the analysis:

1. The significance of including the trend term (γt) without including the specific calendar-year effects (β_t). The null hypothesis is no trend.[8]

2. The joint significance of including the specific calendar-year effects, but no trend term. The null hypothesis is no year-to-year variation.

3. The joint significance of including the year effects when the trend term is also included.[9] The null hypothesis is no year-to-year variation net of the trend.

The estimated trend coefficient and the probability values for the above three significance tests are presented in the first table for each country in Chapter 5.

Also presented from the first stage of the analysis are graphs for each outcome, each country, and each sample used (total, urban, and rural) that chart the year-to-year variation in the predicted values of the dependent variable of the particular equation, based on the models used to conduct the

---

[8]The focus of our analysis is on variation around trend rather than the trend itself. Thus, the trend estimates given in this report should not necessarily be interpreted as best estimates of underlying demographic change. See Appendix B for a discussion of the data quality issues involved.

[9]When the trend is included, one of the calendar-year dummy variables is omitted.

second test listed above. These predicted values are normalized on the basis of their average value over time and presented as variations around zero. Similar graphs of the year-to-year variation of the normalized values of the logarithms of real gross domestic product (GDP) per capita are presented for each country, so that a visual comparison of variation of the economic indicator and of the demographic outcomes can be made.[10] In the cases of marriage and fertility, in which the predicted values are of the log odds of the events occurring, positive correlation of the patterns is expected, that is, improvements in economic conditions are expected to be associated with increases in the probabilities of getting married and giving birth. In the case of mortality, in which the predicted values are of the logarithm of the risk of dying, negative correlation is expected, that is, improvements in the economy should be associated with declines in child mortality.

In the second stage of each of the analyses, the logarithms of economic indicators and their lagged values are substituted for the calendar-year effects in the regressions, which continue to include the trend variable. Separate equations are estimated for each demographic outcome in each country by each economic indicator. The joint significance of the coefficients of the current and lagged values of each economic variable both as a group and in sum is then examined.[11]

Also reported are each of the coefficients on the current and lagged economic indicators, whether or not they are individually significantly different from zero, and the sum of the three coefficients. The individual coefficient estimates should be interpreted with great care because the estimates are likely to be negatively correlated with each other, given the strong autocorrelation in the time series of the economic variables. Nevertheless, some explanation of the meaning of the coefficients is in order. In the cases of marriage and first and second births, for example, a coefficient of 0.05 would indicate that a 100 percent increase in the economic indicator results in a 5 percent increase in the odds of getting married or giving birth.[12] In the case of the mortality analysis, the implication would be a 5 percent increase in the mortality rate.[13]

We turn now to a country-by-country review of economic conditions over time and the presentation of the results of our analysis.

---

[10]For countries for which results are presented for urban and rural samples, as well as for the total sample, the graphs of per capita GDP are for the entire country for all graphs.

[11]It could be that the economic variables would have significant effects, even if there are no calendar-year effects.

[12]Suppose that q_{it}, the probability of individual i getting married in year t, is .1000. Then the odds $[q_{it}/(1 - q_{it})]$ are 0.1111. A 5 percent increase in the odds to 0.1167 implies an increase in q_{it} to .1045.

[13]Suppose that the mortality rate is $h_{iat} = .0100$, then h_{iat} would increase to .0105.

5

Country Results

This chapter presents for each of the seven study countries a description of economic experience in recent decades and the results of our analysis of the effects of that experience on child deaths, first marriages, and first and second births.

BOTSWANA

Economic Experience

Botswana is currently the richest of the seven countries in our sample, with 1987 gross national product (GNP) per capita of $1,050 (World Bank, 1989b). Compared with most other sub-Saharan African countries, Botswana relies little on agriculture for its income. In 1987, agriculture accounted for only 3 percent of gross domestic product (GDP), industry (including mineral extraction) accounted for 57 percent, and services for 40 percent. Even so, 70 percent of the labor force was employed in agriculture in 1980 (World Bank, 1989b). The main agricultural products are livestock, sorghum, maize, and root crops (Central Intelligence Agency, 1989). Mining is the major industrial activity, accounting for 50 percent of GDP in 1988 (Central Intelligence Agency, 1989). Botswana is a major diamond producer and also produces and exports copper and nickel.

Botswana is the only country in our sample that has displayed strong and consistent growth through the last three decades (see Figure 5-1 for changes in GDP per capita). Furthermore, the structure of Botswana's economy has changed drastically over this period. In the 1960s, the economy was based largely on production of crops and cattle. Then, in 1967 the first diamond mine began producing. Other mines were opened in 1969 and 1982 (Hill and Mokgethi, 1989). The share of GDP accounted for by industry (which includes mining) rose from 19 percent in 1965 to 57 percent in 1987 (World Bank, 1989b). Government revenues based on minerals also increased rapidly, growing from 13 percent of total government revenue in 1974-1975 to 54 percent in 1985-1986 (Hill and Mokgethi, 1989).

Fluctuations in the price of diamonds are an important source of fluctuations in the income of Botswana. Because of the high degree of heterogeneity of diamonds, no standard price series is available. According to an index of real unit value for diamonds, diamond prices rose rapidly between 1978 and 1980, fell for the next two years, and then again rose rapidly between 1982 and 1985 (see Hill and Mokgethi, 1989). The slowing of Botswana's growth in the first years of the 1980s, along with the sharp increase in per capita GDP in 1985, reflects these movements in diamond prices.

The policies the government of Botswana has followed since diamond mining began have been aimed at avoiding a buildup of debt and stabilizing growth. Hill and Mokgethi (1989) found that during times of exceptionally high diamond prices, the government saved a substantial portion of the windfall gain in government revenues (in the form of foreign reserves) rather than increasing expenditures. Likewise, when diamond prices fell in the early 1980s, government expenditures were not greatly curtailed. This type of policy buffers consumers from shocks due to changes in commodity prices.

There is little evidence on the distribution of income in Botswana. The imbalance between the share of the labor force that agriculture employs and the share of GDP it produces suggests that income may be unequally distributed. However, central government expenditures on education, health, and social services have increased rapidly since 1972 (World Bank, 1989b). For example, the share of gross national product allocated to public health expenditure rose from 2.02 percent in 1972 to 2.80 percent in 1987. Coupled with an increase in per capita income of more than 7 percent per year over this period, the increased share implies large increases in health expenditures per person. Furthermore, since the early 1980s, the government has run a large-scale food security program that aims to insulate rural households from the adverse effects of drought, as well as generally to improve the nutrition of poor rural children. These pieces of evidence suggest that rural living standards have risen. However, any conclusions about how well various groups are doing await more comprehensive information on the distribution of both private incomes and government expenditures.

In summary, the economic data indicate steady increases in average living standards in Botswana, although it is not clear whether rural and urban living standards are growing at similar rates. The prices of minerals that Botswana exports have experienced some fairly extreme fluctuations over the past decade, producing fluctuations in GDP. However, the government appears to have managed booms and busts so as to minimize their effects on living standards.

In what follows, we analyze the effects of movements in GDP per capita on demographic outcomes in Botswana. Time-series data are not available for other economic indicators. Our analysis is also restricted to the total samples of children and of women from the Demographic and Health Survey (DHS) taken in 1988 because data on urban-rural residence necessary for our analysis were not collected.[1] Moreover, because Botswana has not experienced prolonged or severe fluctuations in living standards (net of trend) and has also managed economic fluctuations well, no strong relationships between GDP per capita and the demographic outcomes are likely to be found.

Demographic Outcomes

Botswana is one of the few sub-Saharan African populations that have made substantial progress in demographic transition in recent decades. The infant mortality rate in the mid-1980s is thought to have been as low as 30 to 40 deaths per 1,000 live births (Hill, 1993), while the total fertility rate in the late 1980s was 4.9 children per woman (Cohen, 1993). Botswana is known for its late age at marriage in comparison with the rest of sub-Saharan Africa (van de Walle, 1993), even though the estimate of the singulate mean age of marriage from the 1988 Demographic and Health Survey is only 17.4 years.

The decline in infant and child mortality as estimated in our analysis is shown in Figure 5-1. The mortality graph charts the deviations in the log of the estimated risks that resulted from a Poisson regression that included as explanatory variables the age of the child and dummy variables for each calendar year. Although the path is not smooth, the decline in mortality is clear, and our analysis indicates that it was indeed significant (see Table 5-1). There were no statistically significant year-to-year variations around the trend from 1970 to 1987, however.

Furthermore, given the steady economic growth in Botswana in recent decades, the absence of any effect of the logarithm of GDP per capita on infant and child mortality, once the time trend is taken into consideration, is

---

[1]For the child mortality analysis, information on the mother's length of residence in current place is required and for the marriage and fertility analysis information on the woman's residence at age 12.

not surprising (see Table 5-2). The probability values (*p*-values) for the tests of significance of the coefficients on GDP and its lagged values, as a group and in sum, are both substantially greater than .10, the cutoff that we use in distinguishing significance. This result does not mean that the secular decline in mortality has not been associated with the increase in GDP in recent decades. It implies merely that the year-to-year variations around the trend of the logarithm of GDP per capita have not been related to the year-to-year variations in mortality.

Figure 5-1 also charts the deviations of the log odds of marrying, based on a model with age of woman and dummy variables for each calendar year; it indicates that the odds of marriage have declined since 1975. The results in Table 5-1 confirm a downward trend in the log odds of marriage for the entire period from 1960 to 1987 and indicate the significant variation around that trend. Moreover, the results in Table 5-2 suggest that the logarithm of GDP per capita was positively associated with the probability of marriage, net of trend. That is, although the odds of marriage have shown a secular decline, year-to-year increases (decreases) in GDP per capita were associated with higher (lower) marriage odds than otherwise expected, as indicated by the coefficients for the current and the one- and two-year lagged values of GDP as a group and in sum. The effect appears to be contemporaneous, with the largest effect at lag 0.

No clear trend over time appears in the first-birth odds in Botswana for the 1960-1987 period (Table 5-1).[2] There were significant variations from year to year, and the probability of having a first birth appears to have been positively associated with GDP per capita (Table 5-2).

The second-birth odds declined over time (Table 5-1), as is apparent since 1980 in Figure 5-1. The significant variations in the rate around the trend were also positively associated with GDP per capita (Table 5-2).

In summary, in Botswana variations in GDP net of trend do not appear to have been related to changes in infant and child mortality in recent years, but they have been positively related to the log odds of marriage and first and second births. These effects are also quite large in comparison to effects that we will see for other countries. However, because Botswana has experienced almost uninterrupted economic progress, this finding certainly does not provide evidence of the demographic effects of economic reversals.

---

[2]When education is introduced into the model, there is a significantly positive trend over time (p = .04). The coefficient on the trend term is 0.01. Thus, once education is allowed for, the log odds of first birth appear to have been increasing over time.

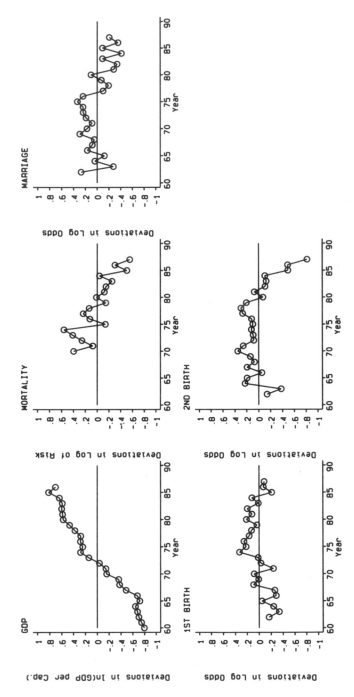

FIGURE 5-1 Time pattern of deviations in the logarithm of real gross domestic product per capita and the estimated demographic outcomes, total sample, Botswana.

TABLE 5-1   Effects of Time Period on Demographic Outcomes, Botswana

	Child Mortality[a]	First Marriage[b]	First Birth[b]	Second Birth[b]
Trend	−.05	−.02	.00	−.03
Tests (*p*-values)[c]				
No trend	.00**	.00**	.16	.00**
No variation	.00**	.00**	.00**	.00**
No variation net of trend	.70	.00**	.00**	.00**
Number				
Children	10,101	—	—	—
Women	—	4,368	4,368	3,227

[a]In mortality analysis, age of child is controlled. Period of analysis is 1970-1987.

[b]In marriage and first-birth analyses, age of woman is controlled; in second-birth analysis, age of woman and interval since first birth are controlled. Period of analysis is 1962-1987.

[c] * indicates a *p*-value of < .10; ** means a *p*-value of < .05.

TABLE 5-2   Effects of Real Gross Domestic Product per Capita on Demographic Outcomes, Botswana

	Child Mortality[a]	First Marriage[b]	First Birth[b]	Second Birth[b]
Coefficients by lag				
0	0.67	1.08**	0.52*	0.54
1	−0.46	0.10	0.40	−0.16
2	0.23	−0.17	0.51	0.87**
Sum of coefficients	0.43	1.02	1.43	1.25
Tests (*p*-values)[c]				
Coefficients are zero	.84	.00**	.00**	.00**
Sum of coefficients is zero	.59	.00**	.00**	.00**

[a]In mortality analysis, age of child is controlled. Period of analysis is 1970-1987.

[b]In marriage and first-birth analyses, age of woman is controlled; in second-birth analysis, age of woman and interval since first birth are controlled. Period of analysis is 1962-1987.

[c] * indicates a *p*-value of < .10; ** means a *p*-value of < .05.

GHANA

Economic Experience

Ghana is classified as a lower-income country, with a 1987 GNP per capita of $390 (World Bank, 1989b). Its economy is based largely on agriculture, which accounted for 51 percent of gross domestic product in 1987 (in contrast with 34 percent for all sub-Saharan countries) and employed 56 percent of the labor force in 1980 (World Bank, 1989b). The main agricultural products are cocoa, coffee, root crops, maize, sorghum, millet, and groundnuts. The major export crop is cocoa, which accounts for 57 percent of the value of total exports in 1982-1984 (Table 2-3). The key role of cocoa is stressed in much of the economic literature on Ghana, as it has employed a substantial share of the population and has been at times a significant source of government revenue.

As shown in Figure 5-2, Ghana experienced a decline in average living standards as measured by real gross domestic product per capita between 1960 and 1988. However, the decline was not continuous. The whole period can be broken, roughly, into a period of slow and uneven growth through 1974, and then a collapse in growth from 1974 through the early 1980s. The years 1983 through 1988 mark the beginning of a still ongoing recovery period.[3]

Independence Through 1974

During this period, the Ghanaian economy was characterized by aggressive import-substitution policies, extensive government intervention in markets for both agricultural exports and consumer goods, and a large expansion of the public sector. The country instituted a program of import restrictions in the early 1960s, and the share in GNP of manufacturing, much of which was conducted by state enterprises, expanded rapidly, from 1.5 percent in 1957 to 10.0 percent in 1966, with a large share of manufacturing conducted by state enterprises. Real producer prices for cocoa declined between 1961 and 1964, and cocoa output and exports fell off in the mid-1960s. The decline in the cocoa sector, and consequent reductions in export revenues, resulted in the largest balance of payments deficit since independence. This imbalance led to restrictions in imports of capital goods, which were necessary for the continued growth of the manufacturing sector, and thus further curtailed the growth of the economy.

The military coup of 1966 marked the beginning of a period of growth for Ghana that persisted through the early 1970s. Aiding the recovery was a

---

[3]For more detailed descriptions of Ghana's economic experience, see Killick (1978) and Younger (1989).

short-lived boom in real world cocoa prices in 1968 and 1969, followed by large price increases in 1973 and 1974. The economic policies of the new political regime also differed somewhat from those of the old and were in general more export oriented. The real producer price of cocoa rose between 1966 and 1968, and the volume of cocoa exports generally increased from 1966 levels. Other changes in policy included a devaluation of the cedi—the Ghanaian currency—in 1966, and a relaxation of import restrictions on consumer goods.

1974 to 1983

The years 1974 through 1983, during which the Ghanaian economy declined, were marked by several policy changes. First, the import controls of the initial postindependence period were revived, as were extensive price controls for consumer goods. Inflation rates increased and did not fall below 50 percent per annum between 1975 and 1980, thus seriously eroding the value of earnings of public sector employees (World Bank, 1991). Second, the volume of exported cocoa declined nearly continuously, from 416,000 metric tons in 1975-1976 to 173,000 metric tons by 1983-1984. The real producer price of cocoa moved erratically because nominal prices were adjusted only sporadically to account for high inflation rates. Smuggling of cocoa to neighboring countries with higher producer prices (Togo and Côte d'Ivoire) became a problem for the Ghanaian government. Although smuggling acted to lower government revenues on (legal) exports, it may also have ameliorated some of the adverse effects of low producer prices for Ghanaian farmers.

The short-lived increase in GDP per capita in the late 1970s can be traced to the boom in export prices (particularly for cocoa) during this time. However, when the terms of trade collapsed in 1980, the Ghanaian economy began to deteriorate markedly. In 1980 and 1981, the Ghanaian government paid cocoa producers prices that were above the low world prices, incurring a loss in government revenue. The effects of the deterioration in the terms of trade were exacerbated by a prolonged and severe drought in the early 1980s, and a food shortage ensued (World Bank, 1991). Moreover, low levels of public expenditure on social infrastructure, particularly on roads and transport, made it difficult to market crops. These two factors combined to cause substantial declines in the output of cereals between 1981 and 1983. The collapse of government revenues also meant a decline in public health services: By 1983, real public expenditure per person on health was only 29 percent of its 1980 value (World Bank, 1989a). The expulsion of approximately 1 million Ghanaians from Nigeria pursuant to the collapse in oil prices exerted additional strain on the economy, increasing urban unemployment.

1983 to 1988

The increase in per capita gross domestic product from 1983 through 1988, shown in Figure 5-2, marks the beginning of a recovery period for Ghana. The economic recovery program of 1983, which was developed in conjunction with the International Monetary Fund and the World Bank, consisted of a classic stabilization package. A major objective of the program was to align prices within Ghana to reflect market conditions. The cedi was devalued, and real producer prices for cocoa were increased 85 percent (in real terms) between 1983 and 1985. Other policy changes included an increase in the wages of civil servants (which had fallen to 10 percent of their 1977 value as a result of the high inflation rates in the late 1970s and early 1980s) and reductions in civil service employment. In addition, the Ghanaian government began investing in key export sectors (cocoa, gold, and timber) and in transport infrastructure. Health expenditures were also increased dramatically; they rose nearly fourfold between 1983 and 1988 (World Bank, 1989a).

In what follows, we investigate whether demographic outcomes in Ghana were affected by a variety of economic indicators. Real GDP per capita provides a measure of overall living standards. We expect it to affect demographic outcomes, although we have no clear hypotheses about how its effects differ in urban and rural areas. We also investigate the link between demographic outcomes and measures of Ghana's terms of trade, its quantity of exports, the world price of cocoa, the quantity of cocoa produced, and the producer price of cocoa. Improvements in the terms of trade and increases in the world price of cocoa should yield increases in living standards, either directly through increases in private sector incomes or indirectly through increases in government revenues and expenditure. Again, we have no clear hypotheses about how the effects of these variables will differ in rural and urban areas. Although rural households may not benefit directly from increases in world cocoa prices (because the producer price they receive is set by the marketing board), they may benefit from increases in government expenditure stimulated by increases in government revenue. The quantity measures (the export quantum index and the measure of cocoa production) should be positively correlated with both private incomes and government revenues, and could affect demographic outcomes in both urban and rural areas.

The producer price of cocoa serves as a measure of rural living standards, and we have particular interest in whether changes in this variable affect rural demographic outcomes. Note, however, that in Ghana, producer prices of cocoa have often moved in the opposite direction from world prices. If rural living standards are positively related to world cocoa prices (as might be expected, given increased government revenue and evidence of smuggling to neighboring countries) the estimated effects of movements in producer prices on demographic outcomes may be seriously biased.

Demographic Outcomes

Child survival improved substantially in the 1950s, 1960s, and 1970s, but in the early 1980s little progress seems to have been made and possibly some reversals occurred (Hill, 1993). There is some indication, however, that in the late 1980s the decline in mortality resumed. Such a pattern of change is consistent with a response of mortality to economic reversals in the early 1980s, as outlined above. The age at marriage for women appears to have increased slowly in recent decades, and in 1988 the singulate mean age at marriage stood at 20.2 years (van de Walle, 1993). Fertility may also have declined slightly, but it remains high by international standards, at an estimated total fertility rate of 6.4 children per woman in the second half of the 1980s (Cohen, 1993).

Figure 5-2 shows how the decline in infant and child mortality stalled in the early 1980s for the population as a whole. The mortality graph charts the deviations of the logarithm of the estimated risks of dying that resulted from a Poisson regression that included as explanatory variables the age of the child and dummy variables for each year.

The pause in mortality decline is also apparent in the mortality graph for the rural sample (see Figure 5-4). The urban pattern, shown in Figure 5-3, is erratic. The results in Table 5-3 indicate, however, that overall there was a significant downward trend in mortality from 1970 to 1987 in the total sample, as well as among children living in urban and rural areas. Only in rural areas was there significant variation around the trend. The probability values for the test of no variation net of trend are .41, .41, and .04 for the total, urban, and rural samples, respectively.

Table 5-4 presents the effects of economic variables on infant and child mortality. Most notable are the results for the effects of the terms of trade (TT) and the world price of cocoa (WPCOC), Ghana's most important export. For these two variables, the effects of the current and lagged logarithmic values either as a group or in sum are significantly negative for both the total and the rural samples.[4] That is, declines in the terms of trade and in the world price of cocoa, both of which were severe in the late 1970s and early 1980s, are associated with increases in child mortality once the trend in mortality is controlled for in rural areas and in the country as a whole.

The log odds of marriage in Ghana fell significantly from 1962 to 1987 for the total and urban samples, but not for women who were residing in

---

[4]The analysis was also conducted separately for each age group. The results were strongest for age groups 10-23 months and 24-35 months, ages in which weaning is likely to take place.

rural areas at age 12 (see Table 5-3). These results are also reflected in Figures 5-2, 5-3, and 5-4. There was no significant year-to-year variation around the trend in the urban or total samples, but there was in the rural. Even so, these variations were not significantly related to the economic variables included in our analysis (see Table 5-5).

For first births, the log odds also significantly declined over time for the total and urban samples, but without significant variation around the trend (Table 5-3). Only the coefficients for the export quantum index (EXQ) and the producer price of cocoa (PPCOC) for the total and rural samples were significantly different from zero, either as a group or in sum; the sums were positive (Table 5-6).

The second-birth odds also declined over time for all three samples in Ghana, but there was no significant variation around the trend (Table 5-3). Once again, in rural areas variation in the export quantum index was associated with this risk (Table 5-7), but the association was negative, an unexpected result. The coefficients on QCOC, cocoa output, did as a group have the hypothesized positive effect on the second-birth odds in rural areas.[5]

Thus for Ghana reversals in terms of trade and the world price of cocoa appear generally to have had the effect of worsening the rates of infant and child mortality relative to the improving trend both for the country as a whole and for rural areas. The export quantum index and the producer price of cocoa also reduced the probabilities of first births in the same areas. The results for second births were mixed, and there were no significant effects on the log odds of marriage. Thus most of the economic variables used in this analysis did not have the hypothesized effects, but a few of the models yielded the expected results. Where effects appeared, people living in rural areas seem to have experienced them more than did those in urban areas.

---

[5]For the rural sample of women, the coefficients on the world price of cocoa (WPCOC) as a group had a positive effect on the log odds of having a second birth once education of the woman was added as a control to the model (p value = .09).

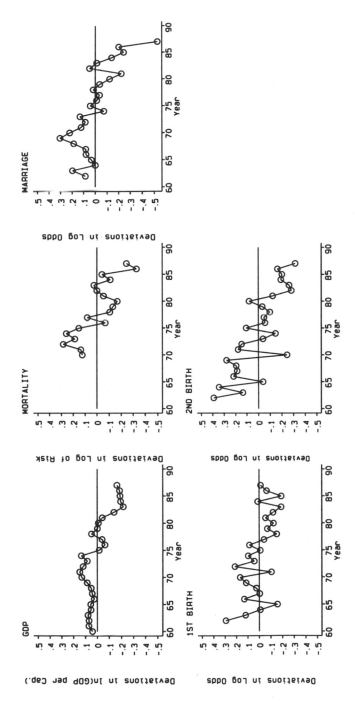

FIGURE 5-2 Time pattern of deviations in the logarithm of real gross domestic product per capita and the estimated demographic outcomes, total sample, Ghana.

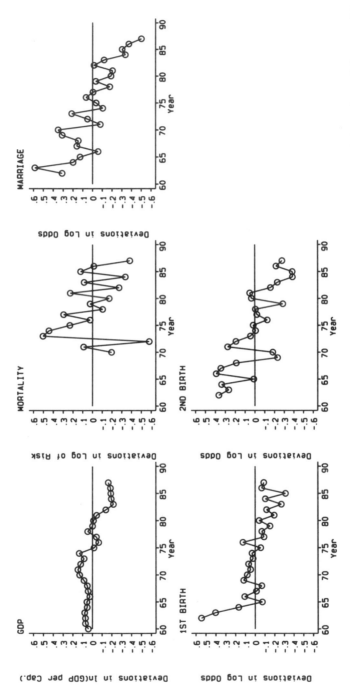

FIGURE 5-3 Time pattern of deviations in the logarithm of real gross domestic product per capita and the estimated demographic outcomes, urban sample, Ghana.

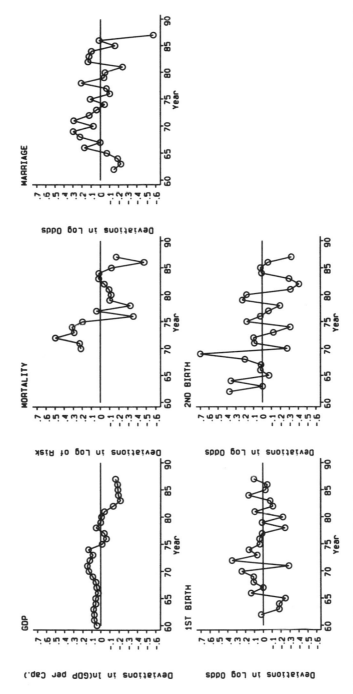

FIGURE 5-4 Time pattern of deviations in the logarithm of real gross domestic product per capita and the estimated demographic outcomes, rural sample, Ghana.

TABLE 5-3   Effects of Time Period on Demographic Outcomes, Ghana

	Child Mortality[a]			First Marriage[b]		
	Total	Urban	Rural	Total	Urban	Rural
Trend	−.03	−.02	−.03	−.02	−.03	−.01
Tests (p-values)[c]						
No trend	.00**	.09*	.00**	.00**	.00**	.12
No variation	.00**	.30	.00**	.00**	.00**	.04**
No variation net of trend	.41	.41	.04**	.12	.68	.05*
Number						
Children	13,957	2,897	7,548	—	—	—
Women	—	—	—	4,476	2,369	2,107

[a]In mortality analysis, age of child is controlled. Period of analysis is 1970-1987.

[b]In marriage and first-birth analyses, age of woman is controlled; in second-birth analysis, age of woman and interval since first birth are controlled. Period of analysis is 1962-1987.

[c] * indicates a p-value of < .10; ** means a p-value of < .05.

TABLE 5-4   Effects of Economic Variables on Child Mortality, Ghana

	GDP			EXQ			TT		
	Total	Urban	Rural	Total	Urban	Rural	Total	Urban	Rural
Coefficients by lag									
0	−0.76	−0.51	−0.82	−0.03	−0.26	0.07	−0.11	0.06	−0.27
1	0.26	0.38	0.62	0.15	0.54	−0.00	−0.14	−0.14	−0.14
2	0.02	0.01	−0.14	0.05	−0.34	0.16	0.01	−0.04	0.06
Sum of coefficients	−0.48	−0.13	−0.34	0.17	−0.06	0.22	−0.24	−0.13	−0.35
Tests (p-values)[a]									
Coefficients are zero	.56	.98	.74	.47	.59	.75	.13	.94	.05*
Sum of coefficients is zero	.52	.94	.72	.32	.89	.32	.04**	.65	.02**

NOTES: Age of child and year are controlled. GDP, real gross domestic product per capita, 1970-1987; EXQ, export quantum index, 1970-1987; TT, terms of trade index, 1970-1987; WPCOC, real world price of cocoa, 1970-1987; QCOC, cocoa output, 1970-1985; PPCOC, real producer price of cocoa, 1970-1985.

[a] * indicates a p-value of < .10; ** means a p-value of < .05.

First Birth[b]			Second Birth[b]		
Total	Urban	Rural	Total	Urban	Rural
−.01	−.02	−.00	−.02	−.02	−.02
.00**	.00**	.88	.00**	.00**	.00**
.09**	.12	.32	.00**	.06*	.02**
.53	.92	.27	.81	.94	.10
—	—	—	—	—	—
4,483	2,372	2,111	3,367	1,725	1,642

WPCOC			QCOC			PPCOC		
Total	Urban	Rural	Total	Urban	Rural	Total	Urban	Rural
−0.01	0.25	−0.12	−0.04	1.26**	−0.15	0.03	0.66	−0.01
−0.03	−0.03	−0.05	−0.36	−1.25	−0.50	−0.04	0.07	−0.10
−0.18	−0.15	−0.24	0.18	1.48*	−0.05	0.02	0.59	0.14
−0.22	0.07	−0.42	−0.22	1.49	−0.69	0.02	1.32	0.03
.07*	.53	.02**	.60	.19	.31	.99	.41	.88
.03**	.76	.00**	.52	.10	.12	.92	.24	.91

TABLE 5-5   Effects of Economic Variables on Marriage, Ghana

	GDP			EXQ			TT		
	Total	Urban	Rural	Total	Urban	Rural	Total	Urban	Rural
Coefficients by lag									
0	−0.24	−0.61	0.10	−0.13	−0.04	−0.24	0.19	0.16	0.21
1	0.32	0.34	0.32	0.06	0.05	0.07	−0.19	−0.24	−0.15
2	0.31	0.46	0.07	0.07	−0.02	0.14	0.12	0.20	0.03
Sum of coefficients	0.40	0.19	0.49	−0.00	−0.00	−0.03	0.12	0.13	0.09
Tests (p-values)[a]									
Coefficients are zero	.38	.46	.76	.43	.99	.20	.40	.62	.63
Sum of coefficients is zero	.24	.69	.32	.99	.98	.88	.19	.33	.50

NOTES: Age of woman and year are controlled. GDP, real gross domestic product per capita, 1962-1987; EXQ, export quantum index, 1962-1987; TT, terms of trade index, 1962-1987; WPCOC, real world price of cocoa, 1962-1987; QCOC, cocoa output, 1962-1985; PPCOC, real producer price of cocoa, 1962-1985.

[a] * indicates a p-value of < .10; ** means a p-value of < .05.

TABLE 5-6   Effects of Economic Variables on First Births, Ghana

	GDP			EXQ			TT		
	Total	Urban	Rural	Total	Urban	Rural	Total	Urban	Rural
Coefficients by lag									
0	0.31	0.37	0.20	0.24**	0.09	0.40**	0.06	0.10	−0.00
1	−0.34	−0.70	0.02	−0.14	0.03	−0.32	−0.19	−0.21	−0.18
2	0.25	0.35	0.11	0.15	−0.05	0.34**	0.07	0.12	−0.01
Sum of coefficients	0.21	0.02	0.32	0.24	0.08	0.41	−0.07	0.01	−0.19
Tests (p-values)[a]									
Coefficients are zero	.87	.85	.93	.14	.82	.05*	.53	.84	.42
Sum of coefficients is zero	.53	.97	.52	.04**	.65	.02**	.45	.93	.17

NOTES: Age of woman and year are controlled. GDP, real gross domestic product per capita, 1962-1987; EXQ, export quantum index, 1962-1987; TT, terms of trade index, 1962-1987; WPCOC, real world price of cocoa, 1962-1987; QCOC, cocoa output, 1962-1985; PPCOC, real producer price of cocoa, 1962-1985.

[a] * indicates a p-value of < .10; ** means a p-value of < .05.

WPCOC			QCOC			PPCOC		
Total	Urban	Rural	Total	Urban	Rural	Total	Urban	Rural
0.10	0.18	0.01	−0.10	−0.19	−0.02	−0.08	−0.08	−0.08
−0.02	−0.16	0.13	−0.04	0.15	−0.26	0.18	0.19	0.16
0.01	0.09	−0.09	0.10	−0.06	0.24	−0.09	−0.10	−0.07
0.09	0.11	0.05	−0.04	−0.10	−0.04	0.01	0.01	0.00
.50	.52	.67	.82	.87	.69	.41	.65	.81
.24	.33	.64	.79	.65	.86	.73	.85	.96

WPCOC			QCOC			PPCOC		
Total	Urban	Rural	Total	Urban	Rural	Total	Urban	Rural
0.07	0.02	0.12	0.14	0.10	0.17	0.15**	−0.00	0.32**
−0.15	−0.11	−0.20	−0.09	−0.04	−0.15	−0.22*	−0.02	−0.43**
0.02	0.07	−0.05	0.14	0.11	0.15	0.14	0.08	0.19
−0.06	−0.01	0.13	0.19	0.18	0.17	0.07	0.05	0.09
.44	.89	.23	.68	.89	.86	.11	.76	.03**
.46	.90	.26	.25	.44	.49	.07*	.35	.15

TABLE 5-7   Effects of Economic Variables on Second Births, Ghana

	GDP			EXQ			TT		
	Total	Urban	Rural	Total	Urban	Rural	Total	Urban	Rural
Coefficients by lag									
0	−0.27	0.13	−0.62	−0.00	−0.01	0.02	0.04	0.04	0.01
1	0.76	0.24	1.26	−0.11	0.24	−0.50*	−0.04	−0.25	0.18
2	−0.50	0.23	−1.31*	−0.05	−0.22	0.08	0.15	0.33	−0.02
Sum of coefficients	−0.01	0.59	−0.67	−0.17	0.01	−0.40	0.15	0.13	0.17
Tests (p-values)[a]									
Coefficients are zero	.75	.80	.38	.59	.59	.05*	.57	.44	.68
Sum of coefficients is zero	.99	.34	.30	.27	.95	.07*	.22	.43	.34

NOTES: Age of woman, interval since first birth, and year are controlled. GDP, real gross domestic product per capita, 1962-1987; EXQ, export quantum index, 1962-1987; TT, terms of trade index, 1962-1987; WPCOC, real world price of cocoa, 1962-1987; QCOC, cocoa output, 1962-1985; PPCOC, real producer price of cocoa, 1962-1985.

[a] * indicates a p-value of < .10; ** means a p-value of < .05.

WPCOC			QCOC			PPCOC		
Total	Urban	Rural	Total	Urban	Rural	Total	Urban	Rural
0.01	−0.07	0.08	0.33	−0.13	0.80**	0.06	−0.05	0.18
−0.01	−0.05	0.02	−0.14	−0.15	−0.38	−0.03	0.06	−0.14
0.11	0.11	0.13	0.03	0.31	−0.32	−0.01	0.03	−0.04
0.11	−0.01	0.23	0.23	0.33	0.10	0.02	0.04	−0.01
.66	.79	.45	.49	.40	.02**	.93	.88	.53
.29	.94	.11	.30	.28	.75	.69	.59	.94

KENYA

Economic Experience

Kenya's GNP per capita of $330 was slightly lower than that of Ghana in 1987 (World Bank, 1989b), but its economy is more diversified: Agriculture accounts for 31 percent of GDP, industry for 19 percent, and services for the rest. Four-fifths of the labor force worked in agriculture in 1980 (World Bank, 1989b). Kenya's major food crops include maize, wheat, sugar, and rice, and its major exports are coffee, tea, and refined petroleum products. These last are made from imported crude petroleum, with relatively little value added. Tourism has also emerged as a strong source of employment for Kenya; it is the major source of foreign exchange earnings from services (World Bank, 1983).

The Kenyan pattern of growth in per capita income between the early 1960s and 1985 is typical of many African countries. As shown in Figure 5-5, Kenya experienced relatively high rates of growth in per capita GDP between the early 1960s and the early 1970s, little growth through 1980, and declines in the first half of the 1980s. Much of the movement in average Kenyan living standards over this time period can be explained by international factors and the Kenyan government's responses to them. However, drought, general economic policies, and political instability may also have been important determinants of living standards at times.

1963 to 1973

The high-growth period in Kenya, covering roughly 1963 to 1973, was characterized by rapid expansion in both the agricultural sector and the smaller industrial sector. The value of agricultural output grew at an average rate of 6.2 percent per annum between 1965 and 1973 and the value of industrial output grew at 12.4 percent; both rates were substantially greater than the rate of population growth, which was roughly 3.4 percent per year (World Bank, 1989b). Services, including tourism, also grew rapidly, at 7.6 percent per year.

The high rates of growth in agriculture have been attributed to the transfer of high-quality land to smallholders (Tostensen and Scott, 1987); the adoption of high-yield maize varieties; and the expansion of coffee, tea, and dairy production (World Bank, 1983). Overall, the highest growth rates in agriculture occurred in the export-oriented subsector (coffee and tea). Industrial growth was fostered by the expansion of domestic demand, protectionist policies toward manufactured imports, government participation in industrial projects, and growth in foreign investment (World Bank, 1983; Godfrey, 1986).

The high growth rates in all sectors during the 1965-1973 period imply increases in the average Kenyan standard of living. However, according to sketchy evidence on the distribution of real per capita income, not all individuals may have benefited substantially during this period. A 1983 World Bank study concludes that poverty was then, and continues to be, largely a rural phenomenon, with only 3 to 6 percent of urban individuals below the poverty line in 1974. At the same time, more than a third of smallholders, pastoralists, migrant farmers, and farm squatters lived in poverty; the highest rate was 85 percent, for pastoralists. Poverty rates among smallholders are of special concern because this group accounted for 70 percent of the population in 1974. The study also noted that the proportion of smallholders below the poverty line appears to have declined somewhat during the 1960s. However, the distribution of rural incomes seems to have worsened: Between 1963 and 1974, the poorest 40 percent experienced no gains in income (World Bank, 1983). That a large fraction of the population saw no improvement in income can be reconciled with high growth rates in agriculture: Much of that growth was in coffee and tea, and only 27 percent and 12 percent of smallholders, respectively, raised these crops in 1974. These pieces of evidence are sketchy; they come from only two provinces. However, taken together, they do suggest that a large proportion of Kenyans gained little from the high growth years of the 1960s and early 1970s.

1973 to 1980

For several reasons the growth of per capita income in Kenya was quite slow between 1973 and 1980 (see Figure 5-5). The oil shock of 1973 adversely affected industrial development and resulted in a large balance of payments deficit. The collapse of the East African Community limited Kenya's markets for manufactures. The growth in the value of industrial output fell to 5.7 percent per year during 1973-1980. Agriculture, as well, experienced a slowdown in its growth rate, which averaged 3.7 percent per year between 1973 and 1980, less than the estimated 3.8 percent rate of population growth during this period. This slowing of growth in agriculture has been attributed to poor weather, the lack of new high-quality land on which to expand production, and the halt in technical progress in seed varieties (World Bank, 1983). Government intervention in the pricing of maize, wheat, milk, meat, sugarcane, and cotton has also been mentioned as a factor (Tostensen and Scott, 1987).

Although growth was slow on average over the 1973-1980 period, it was not uniformly so. In particular, the 1976-1977 boom in coffee prices boosted incomes. The coffee price that producers in Kenya receive closely mirrors the world price, so this boom must have had significant effects on incomes for coffee-growing smallholders.

1978 On

The period 1978-1980 marked the beginning of a decline in per capita income that continued to 1985. A number of reasons underlay this decline. First, the coffee boom ended, and real world prices fell 43 percent between 1977 and 1978, and 19 percent between 1979 and 1980. Tea prices also declined. Two factors exacerbated the effect of these declines: First, a severe drought in 1979 curtailed maize production and led to urban food shortages that required emergency food imports. Second, the 1979 increase in oil prices further worsened Kenya's terms of trade. Together, these factors resulted in an increasingly large current account deficit, which amounted to over 14 percent of GDP by 1980 (World Bank, 1983).

The years 1980-1988 were ones of stabilization and structural adjustment. A series of devaluations eroded the dollar value of the shilling 52 percent between 1980 and 1984 (Godfrey, 1986). The current account deficit was reduced to 3.5 percent of GDP by 1985 (World Bank, 1989b). Real wages fell, with the official minimum wage declining 36 percent in real terms between 1980 and 1984. Prices paid to farmers for cereals were increased sharply, and, with the exception of the 1984 drought year, agricultural output began to grow relatively quickly so that its share in GDP actually increased slightly between 1980 and 1986. Despite these changes, per capita income declined between 1980 and 1985, and it increased only a little between 1985 and 1988. Continuing declines in the prices of the major commodity exports of coffee and tea were one source of the weakness in the economy during this period.

In what follows, we examine the relationship between demographic outcomes and several economic indicators. These indicators include real per capita GDP, indices of the terms of trade and export quantities, the world prices of coffee and tea, and the producer price of coffee. The first three measures are general indicators of economic performance, and we expect them to affect demographic outcomes in both urban and rural areas. Because Kenya allows the world and producer prices of coffee to move together, we do not expect the demographic effects of these two variables to differ substantially, in either urban or rural areas. Movements of coffee and tea prices should affect both the incomes of coffee and tea producers and government revenues through taxes. Therefore, price increases might have urban demographic effects, due to additional government expenditures, as well as rural effects, due to increases both in rural incomes and in government expenditures. However, given the diversity of the Kenyan economy and the fact that many rural households produce no coffee or tea, movements in these prices might have only indirect effects on living standards.

Demographic Outcomes

Kenya, like Botswana, is one of the few sub-Saharan African countries to have made substantial progress in its demographic transition. The total fertility rate fell from about 8.0 children per woman in the late 1970s to 6.7 in the late 1980s (Cohen, 1993), but comparison of data from the DHS and the earlier World Fertility Survey indicates that age at marriage has changed little (van de Walle, 1993). Hill (1993) estimates that the probability of dying by age 5 was halved between 1945 and 1985.

Figure 5-5 and Table 5-8 indicate that mortality indeed decreased between 1970 and 1988, but if characteristics of the child and mother are controlled, as discussed in Chapter 4, there was no significant trend.[6] However, there have been significant variations, no matter what the model. Even so, the results in Table 5-9 reveal no clear significant association between changes in economic conditions and mortality. The terms of trade and the world price of tea were negatively associated with child mortality, but the export quantum index had a perverse positive effect. The coefficients on the other three economic indicators did not have effects, either as a group or in sum.[7]

There was a negative trend in the risk of marriage for the total, urban, and rural samples in Kenya from 1962 to 1987, as well as significant variation around the trend (Table 5-8 and Figures 5-5, 5-6, and 5-7). The following economic variables had the hypothesized positive effects on the probability of marriage for the indicated samples: GDP, total and rural; EXQ, total, urban, and rural; and real producer price of coffee (PPCOF), rural (Table 5-10). The world price of tea had a *negative* effect on marriage in all three samples.[8]

There was a negative trend in the log odds of first birth and significant variation around that trend for women who lived in rural areas at age 12 and for the sample as a whole, but not for the urban sample (Table 5-8). GDP and EXQ had positive effects in all three samples, whereas the real world price of coffee (WPCOF) had positive effects only for the urban sample and PPCOF for the total and urban samples (Table 5-11). TT and the real world price of tea (WPTEA) had perverse negative effects.

---

[6]Given the relatively small urban population in Kenya, it was not possible to carry out the mortality analysis separately for the urban and rural samples of children.

[7]The coefficients on the world price of coffee (WPCOF) in sum (–0.18) are significantly negative in a model with control variables ($p = .09$).

[8]In models with a control for education, there are additional significant effects: GDP in sum, total ($p = .08$); WPCOF as a group and in sum, total ($p = .07$ and .06, respectively); WPCOF as a group and in sum, rural ($p = .08$ and .04, respectively); WPTEA as a group, rural ($p = .09$); and PPCOF in sum, total ($p = .07$). The signs of the sums in these cases are not different from those in Table 5-10.

Although there was a negative trend in the log odds of second births in all three samples, no significant variation around the trend was found (Table 5-8). Of the economic variables, only TT for the urban sample had coefficients that were significantly positive in sum; however, the effect was very large (Table 5-12).

Given these mixed negative and positive results, it is difficult to reach a strong conclusion about whether variations in economic conditions net of trends have significantly influenced demographic outcomes in Kenya. This difficulty is not surprising for two reasons: The economic crisis was not severe in Kenya, and the Kenyan economy is quite diverse by sub-Saharan African standards. Accordingly, changes in the prices of one commodity were not likely to have significant effects on large segments of the population. However, real per capita income, which of all the economic indicators used here may come closest to reflecting overall economic well-being, indeed had the hypothesized effects for marriage in the total and rural samples and for first births in all three samples.

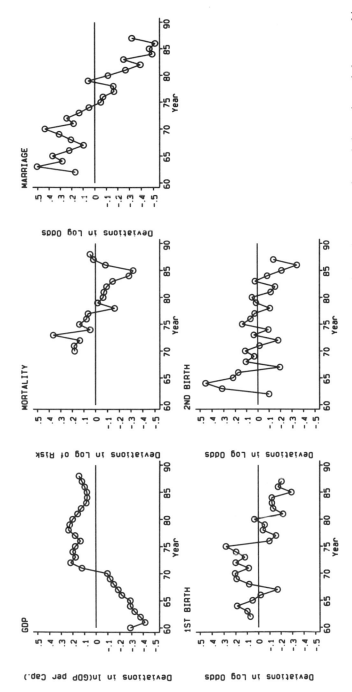

FIGURE 5-5 Time pattern of deviations in the logarithm of real gross domestic product per capita and the estimated demographic outcomes, total sample, Kenya.

TABLE 5-8 Effects of Time Period on Demographic Outcomes, Kenya

	Child Mortality[a]			First Marriage[b]			First Birth[b]			Second Birth[b]		
	Total	Urban	Rural	Total	Urban	Rural	Total	Urban	Rural	Total	Urban	Rural
Trend	-.02	—	—	-.04	-.03	-.04	-.02	-.01	-.01	-.01	-.03	.01
Tests (p-values)[c]												
No trend	.00**	—	—	.00**	.00**	.00**	.00**	.12	.00**	.00**	.01**	.00**
No variation	.00**	—	—	.00**	.00**	.00**	.00**	.29	.00**	.00**	.11	.01**
No variation net of trend	.04**	—	—	.00**	.06*	.00**	.00**	.38	.00**	.12	.34	.11
Number												
Children	24,769	—	—	—	—	—						
Women	—	—	—	7,125	1,105	6,020	7,145	1,108	6,037	5,362	762	4,600

[a]In mortality analysis, age of child is controlled. Period of analysis is 1970-1988.

[b]In marriage and first-birth analyses, age of woman is controlled; in second-birth analysis, age of woman and interval since first birth are controlled. Period of analysis is 1962-1987.

[c] * indicates a p-value of < .10; ** means a p-value of < .05.

TABLE 5-9 Effects of Economic Variables on Child Mortality, Kenya

	GDP Total	EXQ Total	TT Total	WPCOF Total	WPTEA Total	PPCOF Total
Coefficients by lag						
0	-0.19	0.60**	-0.36	-0.08	-0.22*	-0.01
1	1.01	0.06	-0.37	-0.09	-0.30**	-0.12
2	-0.87*	0.08	0.04	0.01	0.07	-0.00
Sum of coefficients	-0.04	0.74	-0.69	-0.16	-0.45	-0.13
Tests (p-values)[a]						
Coefficients are zero	.29	.01**	.02**	.36	.01**	.47
Sum of coefficients is zero	.87	.00**	.02**	.12	.03**	.21

NOTES: Age of child and year are controlled. GDP, real gross domestic product per capita, 1970-1988; EXQ, export quantum index, 1970-1988; TT, terms of trade index, 1970-1988; WPCOF, real world price of coffee, 1970-1987; WPTEA, real world price of tea, 1970-1987; PPCOF, real producer price of coffee, 1970-1987.

[a] * indicates a p-value of < .10; ** means a p-value of < .05.

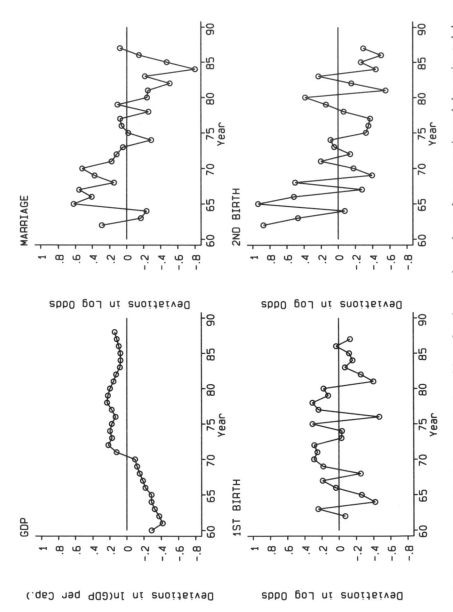

FIGURE 5-6 Time pattern of deviations in the logarithm of real gross domestic product per capita and the estimated demographic outcomes, urban sample, Kenya.

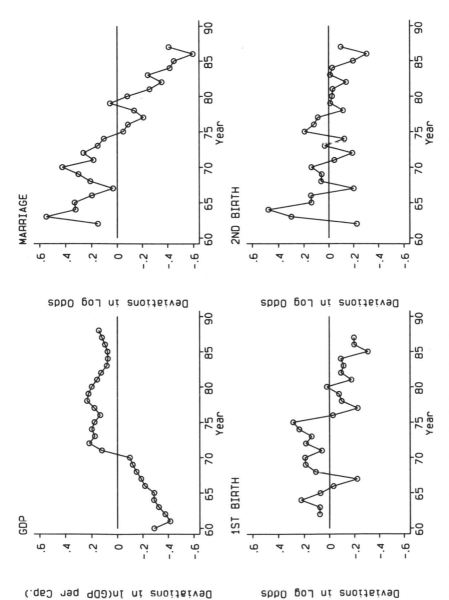

FIGURE 5-7 Time pattern of deviations in the logarithm of real gross domestic product per capita and the estimated demographic outcomes, rural sample, Kenya.

TABLE 5-10   Effects of Economic Variables on Marriage, Kenya

	GDP			EXQ			TT		
	Total	Urban	Rural	Total	Urban	Rural	Total	Urban	Rural
Coefficients by lag									
0	−0.03	0.04	−0.04	0.06	0.84**	−0.09	−0.14	−0.65	−0.04
1	1.18**	1.30	1.17**	0.32*	0.30	0.33	−0.23	−0.20	−0.24
2	−0.99**	−1.73**	−0.84**	−0.04	−0.47	0.07	0.27	−0.07	0.33
Sum of coefficients	0.17	−0.39	0.29	0.35	0.67	0.30	−0.10	−0.92	0.05
Tests (p-values)[a]									
Coefficients are zero	.00**	.17	.00**	.01**	.05*	.02**	.26	.30	.39
Sum of coefficients is zero	.23	.30	.06*	.00**	.03**	.01**	.68	.13	.84

NOTES: Age of woman and year are controlled. GDP, real gross domestic product per capita, 1962-1987; EXQ, export quantum index, 1962-1987; TT, terms of trade index, 1962-1987; WPCOF, real world price of coffee, 1962-1987; WPTEA, real world price of tea, 1962-1987; PPCOF, real producer price of coffee, 1962-1987.

[a] * indicates a p-value of < .10; ** means a p-value of < .05.

TABLE 5-11   Effects of Economic Variables on First Births, Kenya

	GDP			EXQ			TT		
	Total	Urban	Rural	Total	Urban	Rural	Total	Urban	Rural
Coefficients by lag									
0	0.20	2.13**	−0.09	0.18	0.50	0.13	−0.26	0.19	−0.35
1	0.51	−0.87	0.72	−0.06	−0.07	−0.05	−0.23	0.51	−0.38
2	−0.26	−0.69	−0.16	0.25*	0.31	0.25	0.09	−0.36	0.17
Sum of coefficients	0.45	0.57	0.47	0.37	0.73	0.33	−0.41	0.34	−0.55
Tests (p-values)[a]									
Coefficients are zero	.00**	.02**	.00**	.00**	.12	.02**	.11	.58	.02**
Sum of coefficients is zero	.00**	.13	.00**	.00**	.02**	.00**	.08*	.57	.03**

NOTES: Age of woman and year are controlled. GDP, real gross domestic product per capita, 1962-1987; EXQ, export quantum index, 1962-1987; TT, terms of trade index, 1962-1987; WPCOF, real world price of coffee, 1962-1987; WPTEA, real world price of tea, 1962-1987; PPCOF, real producer price of coffee, 1962-1987.

[a] * indicates a p-value of < .10; ** means a p-value of < .05.

WPCOF			WPTEA			PPCOF		
Total	Urban	Rural	Total	Urban	Rural	Total	Urban	Rural
−0.02	−0.11	−0.00	−0.20**	−0.34	−0.17*	−0.02	−0.04	−0.01
−0.02	0.03	−0.03	−0.13	−0.35	−0.09	0.04	0.12	0.03
0.15**	0.10	0.16**	0.05	0.41*	−0.04	0.04	−0.17	0.09
0.11	0.02	0.13	−0.29	−0.28	−0.31	0.07	−0.09	0.10
.12	.82	.14	.01**	.01**	.10	.57	.81	.27
.15	.91	.11	.03**	.38	.03**	.22	.50	.08*

WPCOF			WPTEA			PPCOF		
Total	Urban	Rural	Total	Urban	Rural	Total	Urban	Rural
−0.06	−0.04	−0.06	−0.17*	−0.00	−0.20**	0.02	−0.00	0.03
−0.00	0.42*	−0.09	−0.14	0.12	−0.20*	−0.00	0.46*	−0.09
0.03	−0.07	0.05	−0.13	0.03	−0.16	0.08	−0.22	0.14*
−0.03	0.32	−0.10	−0.45	0.14	−0.56	0.10	0.23	0.09
.69	.08*	.31	.00**	.94	.00**	.26	.06*	.26
.64	.08*	.22	.00**	.66	.00**	.05*	.09*	.14

TABLE 5-12   Effects of Economic Variables on Second Births, Kenya

	GDP			EXQ			TT		
	Total	Urban	Rural	Total	Urban	Rural	Total	Urban	Rural
Coefficients by lag									
0	−0.79*	−0.68	−0.82*	−0.20	−0.92*	−0.10	0.27	0.06	0.28
1	0.48	0.25	0.50	0.05	−0.13	0.08	−0.44	0.40	−0.55*
2	0.37	0.31	0.38	0.07	0.33	0.01	0.29	1.29**	0.14
Sum of coefficients	0.06	−0.12	0.06	−0.08	−0.71	−0.01	0.12	1.75	−0.14
Tests (p-values)[a]									
Coefficients are zero	.14	.93	.16	.81	.22	.98	.33	.09*	.26
Sum of coefficients is zero	.75	.83	.75	.61	.10	.97	.70	.03**	.68

NOTES: Age of woman, interval since first birth, and year are controlled.   GDP, real gross domestic product per capita, 1962-1987; EXQ, export quantum index, 1962-1987; TT, terms of trade index, 1962-1987; WPCOF, real world price of coffee, 1962-1987; WPTEA, real world price of tea, 1962-1987; PPCOF, real producer price of coffee, 1962-1987.

[a] * indicates a p-value of < .10; ** means a p-value of < .05.

WPCOF			WPTEA			PPCOF		
Total	Urban	Rural	Total	Urban	Rural	Total	Urban	Rural
0.11	−0.14	0.14	0.10	−0.00	0.11	−0.01	−0.21	0.02
−0.03	0.07	−0.05	−0.10	0.06	−0.13	−0.03	0.12	−0.06
−0.05	0.19	−0.09	−0.14	0.12	−0.18	0.06	0.13	0.05
0.03	0.12	−0.00	−0.14	0.19	−0.19	0.02	0.03	0.01
.53	.69	.27	.24	.96	.13	.92	.74	.96
.79	.63	.98	.40	.68	.27	.74	.86	.85

NIGERIA

Economic Experience

In 1987, Nigeria had a GNP per capita of $370 (World Bank, 1989b). Agriculture accounted for 30 percent of GDP, and industry (including oil extraction) for 43 percent. Two-thirds of the labor force was in agriculture in 1980. Nigeria grows a wide variety of food crops, and it exports cocoa, palm kernels, and rubber. Since the 1970s, petroleum has dominated the export market, accounting for about 95 percent of total export earnings in the 1980s.

The Nigerian economy has changed considerably over the past three decades. During the 1960s, Nigeria experienced slow, and at times negative, growth per capita (Figure 5-8). In the three years before the 1973 oil price increase, Nigeria's economy began to grow more quickly than it had in the 1960s. The cessation of the 1967-1970 civil war and the expansion of the Nigerian oil industry were likely factors in this growth. The 1973 surge in oil prices further increased growth rates. Export earnings rose rapidly, and much of the increase accrued to the state in the form of government revenues.

Government revenues from oil accounted for 65 percent of total tax revenues in 1978, and 81 percent in 1980 (Gersovitz and Paxson, 1990). The Nigerian government responded to the increase in revenues by increasing expenditures. In nominal terms, government spending increased more than two-and-a-half times between 1973 and 1974 (Kirk-Greene and Rimmer, 1981). Government expenditures rose from less than 20 percent of GDP in 1970-1973 to 35 percent in 1974-1977. The government undertook ambitious public investments, concentrated in urban areas. Expenditure on social services increased as well, so that primary school enrollment rose from 36 percent in 1960 to 62 percent in 1978 (World Bank, 1981). Expenditures grew more quickly than did revenues, and the government experienced deficits throughout the latter half of the 1970s (Kirk-Greene and Rimmer, 1981).

With the rise in oil prices in 1973, economic activity in Nigeria shifted sharply away from agriculture. Exports of cocoa in 1980 were less than half of 1965 quantities, and exports of palm kernels and rubber declined even more (World Bank, 1989b). Production of many food crops also declined. However, the boom in oil prices spurred growth in some sectors of the economy. Construction, which had accounted for 6.4 percent of Nigerian GDP in 1970, climbed to 11.3 percent by 1975.

The downward movements in oil prices in the 1980s produced a sharp decline in per capita GDP, and by 1988 GDP per capita was only 66 percent of that in 1980. Export revenues (as well as government revenues) fell sharply. The government borrowed heavily from foreign sources, and total external debt as a fraction of GNP rose from 5 percent in 1980 to 111 percent in 1987 (World Bank, 1989b). In 1986, the Nigerian government began a liberalization policy, which sought to free exchange rates, reduce trade restrictions and regulations, and remove price controls maintained by government marketing boards. However, none of these policies had substantial effects on output during our sample period.

Some evidence suggests that the rapid growth in the 1970s had little effect on the living standards of the majority of the Nigerian population. Although average incomes rose, rural and informal-sector urban workers realized few benefits, according to Watts and Lubeck (1983). However, data problems make it difficult to draw firm conclusions on changes in the Nigerian income distribution (see Bienen, 1983). Several factors indicate that at least some of the benefits of the oil boom spilled over to poorer segments of the population. First, real central government expenditures on education, health, and social services increased between 1972 and 1980 (World Bank, 1989b). Second, real producer prices for cocoa increased steadily up to 1980, a change that should have benefited rural households.

Several pieces of evidence suggest that the economic decline in the 1980s affected a broad cross section of the Nigerian population. First, some evidence indicates that rural households were adversely affected in the first half of the 1980s. Producer prices for cocoa were lowered drastically between 1980 and 1985, a change that implies a reduction in living standards for some rural households. However, these prices were then increased after 1985 as part of Nigeria's structural adjustment program. The volume of agricultural exports dropped off dramatically in the early 1980s, although it began to rise again in 1984.

Second, cuts in government expenditure resulted in decreases in expenditure for both health and other social services. For example, in 1987, real public health expenditure per person was half what it had been in 1980 (World Bank, 1989b). Nigeria was one of the few countries in sub-Saharan Africa to show a decrease in the percentage of 1-year-old children immunized against DPT (diphtheria, pertussis, and tetanus), polio, and measles between 1981 and 1986-1987 (World Bank, 1989b). There is no information, however, on whether health services deteriorated more in urban or rural areas.

Third, the recession in the 1980s resulted in increases in open unemployment rates in urban areas, especially among younger and more educated workers (see Vandemoortele, 1991). Real wages also fell for both rural and urban civil servants.

In what follows, we investigate the relationship between demographic outcomes and several economic indicators, including per capita GDP, the terms of trade and export quantum index, the world price of crude petroleum, and world and producer prices for cocoa. Movements in the price of crude petroleum (which are also reflected in the terms of trade index) have been the major source of economic fluctuations in Nigeria, and we expect this variable to have significant demographic effects. The evidence discussed above indicates that the effects of the boom in oil prices and the subsequent collapse were felt mostly in urban areas. However, effects on rural areas are also likely. Rural households may have benefited from increases in government expenditures, from remittances from relatives in urban areas, and from a tightening of rural labor markets. Because petroleum is so important to the Nigerian economy and because the downturn in prices in the 1980s was so severe, we expect to find larger demographic effects in Nigeria than we did for economic reversals in other countries.

The producer price of cocoa serves as another measure of rural living standards in Nigeria, and we examine whether it is associated with rural demographic outcomes. It should be noted, however, that between 1985 and 1988, the producer price of cocoa was dramatically increased as part of the structural adjustment program, while GDP per capita was falling. The negative correlation between the two variables in these years could bias our estimates.

Demographic Outcomes

There was little change in child mortality between the mid-1970s and 1990. The probability of dying by age 5 was approximately .190 to .200 in the 1980s (Hill, 1993). Van de Walle (1993) reports no change in the age at marriage in recent decades. Some analysts suggest, however, that fertility decline has begun in some parts of Nigeria (Caldwell et al., 1992), but there is some question at the national level about the accuracy of the count of births in the 1992 Demographic and Health Survey (Federal Office of Statistics, Nigeria, and Institute for Resource Development, 1992; Cohen, 1993).

Our results indicate a downward trend in infant and child mortality from 1970 to 1989, as well as significant variation around the trend (see Figures 5-8, 5-9, and 5-10 and Table 5-13).[9] This variation net of trend was also significantly and negatively associated with changes in the economic variables listed in Table 5-14, especially for the total and urban samples. All the economic variables except the producer price of cocoa have effects on total child mortality. All but PPCOC, EXQ, and the world price of crude petroleum (WPOIL) have effects on urban child mortality.[10]

---

[9]Figure 5-8 suggests that the greatest change in child mortality was before 1975, so that these results are not necessarily inconsistent with the findings of Hill (1993). As noted earlier, our focus in this report is on estimating year-to-year variation rather than on estimating trends.

[10]The last two have negative effects in sum when control variables are added to the models ($p = .08$ for EXQ and $p = .09$ for WPOIL).

For rural children, only TT and WPOIL have significant effects. Thus effects are greater in urban than in rural areas, but the relative effects of the world prices and terms of trade for these two samples are not as great as we might have expected.

The log odds of marriage declined from 1964 to 1989 and there was significant variation around the trend in all three samples of women (see Table 5-13 and Figures 5-8, 5-9, and 5-10).[11] Table 5-15 shows that four of the economic variables (GDP, EXQ, WPCOC, and PPCOC) had coefficients that as a group and in sum had significantly positive effects on marriage in all three samples. The coefficients on the terms of trade (TT) were also significantly different from zero as a group. The results for the world price of crude petroleum are mixed, and the sums of the coefficients are negative for the total and rural samples, contrary to our expectations.[12] Although we are reluctant to emphasize the sign, size, and significance of individual coefficients, it is noteworthy that the biggest effects in the urban sample tend to occur in the current period, whereas they occur with a one-year lag in the rural sample. This pattern is consistent with the effects of economic shocks taking longer to work through the economy to rural areas.

The log odds of first birth also declined in urban Nigeria, but increased in rural areas (Table 5-13 and Figures 5-9 and 5-10).[13] Once again, the economic variables generally had effects in sum (positive) and as a group (Table 5-16).[14] Only for the rural sample did the terms of trade have no effect.

There were no significant trends over time in the log odds of second birth in any of the three samples, although there was significant year-to-year variation (Table 5-13). For the total and rural samples, all the economic variables but the quantity of exports and the producer price of cocoa had positive effects either as a group or in sum (Table 5-17). For the urban sample, only WPCOC and WPOIL had positive effects. For all three samples, the effects of PPCOC were perversely negative.

Altogether then, Nigeria has sustained a heavier impact from economic reversals on all four demographic outcomes than has any other country in our analysis. Moreover, the effects were generally in the hypothesized

---

[11] When the education control is added to the model for urban women, the trend is no longer significantly different from zero ($p = .63$). When the control is added to the total and rural groups, the trend becomes significantly *positive* ($p = .00$ for both).

[12] These two sums are not significantly different from zero in models including education ($p = .48$ for total and $p = .37$ for rural).

[13] In models with education, the trend for the urban sample was insignificant ($p = .16$) and for the total sample, significantly positive ($p = .00$).

[14] For the rural sample, in models with education, the sum of the coefficients on GDP are not significantly different from zero ($p = .32$), and the sum of the coefficients on WPCOC are significantly *negative* ($p = .06$).

directions. The negative effects of petroleum prices on marriage and of the producer price of cocoa on second births are puzzling, but otherwise the results were as expected. Most notable were the effects on variations in the log odds of marriages and first births net of the trends. No doubt the large sample size of the Nigeria DHS had some effect on the statistical significance of the results, but the sample of at least one other country, Kenya, was of comparable size, and the results there were quite weak by comparison. The economy of Nigeria is more heavily dominated by one commodity and the economic shock that was experienced was greater. We believe that these differences are important factors underlying the results of our analysis.

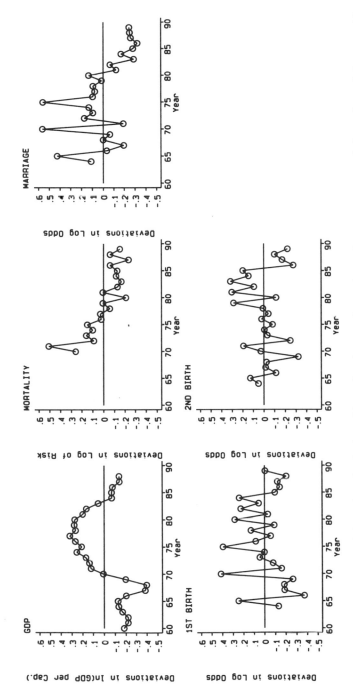

FIGURE 5-8 Time pattern of deviations in the logarithm of real gross domestic product per capita and the estimated demographic outcomes, total sample, Nigeria.

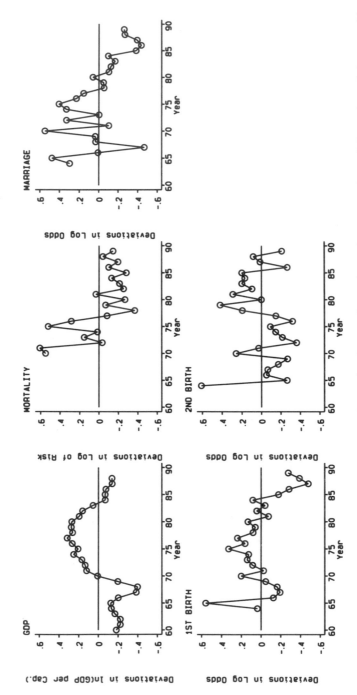

FIGURE 5-9 Time pattern of deviations in the logarithm of real gross domestic product per capita and the estimated demographic outcomes, urban sample, Nigeria.

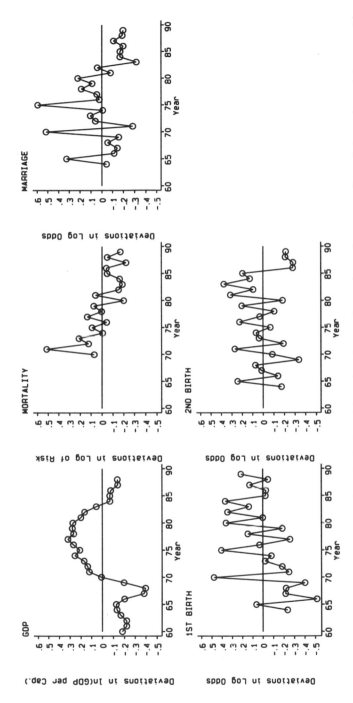

FIGURE 5-10 Time pattern of deviations in the logarithm of real gross domestic product per capita and the estimated demographic outcomes, rural sample, Nigeria.

TABLE 5-13   Effects of Time Period on Demographic Outcomes, Nigeria

	Child Mortality[a]			First Marriage[b]		
	Total	Urban	Rural	Total	Urban	Rural
Trend	−.02	−.03	−.02	−.02	−.03	−.01
Tests (p-values)[c]						
No trend	.00**	.00**	.00**	.00**	.00**	.00**
No variation	.00**	.00**	.00**	.00**	.00**	.00**
No variation net of trend	.00**	.05*	.01**	.00**	.00**	.00**
Number						
Children	28,123	7,844	16,694	—	—	—
Women	—	—	—	8,730	3,524	5,206

[a]In mortality analysis, age of child is controlled. Period of analysis is 1970-1989.

[b]In marriage and first-birth analyses, age of woman is controlled; in second-birth analysis, age of woman and interval since first birth are controlled. Period of analysis is 1964-1989.

[c] * indicates a p-value of < .10; ** means a p-value of < .05.

TABLE 5-14   Effects of Economic Variables on Child Mortality, Nigeria

	GDP			EXQ			TT		
	Total	Urban	Rural	Total	Urban	Rural	Total	Urban	Rural
Coefficients by lag									
0	0.10	−0.34	0.43	−0.12	−0.11	−0.07	−0.14**	−0.20	−0.14*
1	−0.11	0.15	−0.12	0.14	−0.03	0.29*	0.12	0.23	0.13
2	−0.29	−0.51	−0.39	−0.21**	−0.19	−0.25**	−0.13*	−0.29*	−0.12
Sum of coefficients	−0.31	−0.70	−0.08	−0.19	−0.32	−0.04	−0.15	−0.26	−0.13
Tests (p-values)[a]									
Coefficients are zero	.00**	.06*	.15	.02**	.32	.11	.00**	.05**	.04**
Sum of coefficients is zero	.03**	.05**	.66	.02**	.10	.71	.00**	.02**	.02**

NOTES: Age of child and year are controlled. GDP, real gross domestic product per capita, 1970-1988; EXQ, export quantum index, 1970-1988; TT, terms of trade index, 1970-1988; WPCOC, real world price of cocoa, 1970-1987; WPOIL, real world price of crude petroleum, 1970-1987; PPCOC, real producer price of cocoa, 1970-1988.

[a] * indicates a p-value of < .10; ** means a p-value of < .05.

First Birth[b]			Second Birth[b]		
Total	Urban	Rural	Total	Urban	Rural
−.00	−.02	.01	−.00	.01	−.00
.68	.00**	.00**	.64	.28	.20
.00**	.00**	.00**	.00**	.01**	.00**
.00**	.00**	.00**	.00**	.01**	.00**
—	—	—	—	—	—
8,768	3,526	5,242	6,224	?,231	3,993

WPCOC			WPOIL			PPCOC		
Total	Urban	Rural	Total	Urban	Rural	Total	Urban	Rural
−0.14*	−0.25	−0.05	−0.15**	−0.21	−0.17**	0.08	0.10	0.14
0.07	−0.07	0.04	0.14*	0.26	0.17*	−0.03	0.11	−0.14
−0.05	0.04	0.01	−0.09	−0.30	−0.11	0.03	−0.07	0.16
−0.12	−0.28	−0.00	−0.11	−0.25	−0.11	0.08	0.14	0.16
.20	.15	.94	.02**	.18	.05**	.54	.39	.46
.07*	.09*	.95	.11	.12	.17	.45	.56	.20

TABLE 5-15   Effects of Economic Variables on Marriage, Nigeria

	GDP			EXQ			TT		
	Total	Urban	Rural	Total	Urban	Rural	Total	Urban	Rural
Coefficients by lag									
0	0.50**	0.96**	0.23	0.23**	0.41**	0.10	0.13**	0.25**	0.06
1	0.57	−0.15	0.91**	0.09	−0.13	0.20	0.33**	0.16	0.43**
2	−0.63	−0.30	−0.71**	0.01	0.05	0.03	−0.47**	−0.38**	−0.49**
Sum of coefficients	0.44	0.51	0.42	0.33	0.33	0.33	−0.01	0.03	0.01
Tests (p-values)[a]									
Coefficients are zero	.00**	.00**	.00**	.00**	.00**	.00**	.00**	.00**	.00**
Sum of coefficients is zero	.00**	.00**	.00**	.00**	.00**	.00**	.90	.72	.92

NOTES: Age of woman and year are controlled. GDP, real gross domestic product per capita, 1964-1988; EXQ, export quantum index, 1964-1988; TT, terms of trade index, 1964-1988; WPCOC, real world price of cocoa, 1964-1987; WPOIL, real world price of crude petroleum, 1964-1987; PPCOC, real producer price of cocoa, 1964-1988.

[a] * indicates a p-value of < .10; ** means a p-value of < .05.

TABLE 5-16   Effects of Economic Variables on First Births, Nigeria

	GDP			EXQ			TT		
	Total	Urban	Rural	Total	Urban	Rural	Total	Urban	Rural
Coefficients by lag									
0	−0.06	0.48	−0.41	0.04	0.22	−0.06	0.15**	0.20*	0.10
1	0.88**	−0.05	1.41**	0.02	0.02	0.01	0.26**	0.22	0.27**
2	−0.40*	0.31	−0.81**	0.13	0.10	0.13	−0.20**	−0.11	−0.23**
Sum of coefficients	0.42	0.74	0.18	0.20	0.35	0.08	0.22	0.31	0.15
Tests (p-values)[a]									
Coefficients are zero	.00**	.00**	.00**	.00**	.00**	.26	.00**	.00**	.00**
Sum of coefficients is zero	.00**	.00**	.08*	.00**	.00**	.18	.00**	.00**	.02**

NOTES: Age of woman and year are controlled. GDP, real gross domestic product per capita, 1964-1988; EXQ, export quantum index, 1964-1988; TT, terms of trade index, 1964-1988; WPCOC, real world price of cocoa, 1964-1987; WPOIL, real world price of crude petroleum, 1964-1987; PPCOC, real producer price of cocoa, 1964-1988.

[a] * indicates a p-value of < .10; ** means a p-value of < .05.

WPCOC			WPOIL			PPCOC		
Total	Urban	Rural	Total	Urban	Rural	Total	Urban	Rural
−0.19**	0.04	−0.28**	0.09	0.23**	0.02	−0.06	−0.05	−0.08
0.44**	0.12	0.57**	0.21**	0.04	0.29**	0.24**	0.18	0.27**
−0.03	0.05	−0.04	−0.43**	−0.30**	−0.46**	0.22**	0.36**	0.14
0.22	0.22	0.24	−0.14	−0.03	−0.15	0.40	0.49	0.33
.00**	.09*	.00**	.00**	.00**	.00**	.00**	.00**	.00**
.00**	.02**	.00**	.01**	.79	.03**	.00**	.00**	.00**

WPCOC			WPOIL			PPCOC		
Total	Urban	Rural	Total	Urban	Rural	Total	Urban	Rural
−0.24**	0.13	−0.47**	0.14**	0.19**	0.11	−0.23**	−0.21*	−0.25**
0.42**	0.12	0.59**	0.15**	0.17	0.13	0.16*	0.00	0.26**
−0.12*	0.02	−0.22**	−0.21**	−0.16	−0.22**	0.17**	0.41**	0.02
0.06	0.26	−0.10	0.08	0.20	0.02	0.10	0.20	0.03
.00**	.02**	.00**	.00**	.00**	.00**	.00**	.00**	.00**
.35	.01**	.19	.17	.04**	.78	.24	.16	.79

TABLE 5-17   Effects of Economic Variables on Second Births, Nigeria

	GDP			EXQ			TT		
	Total	Urban	Rural	Total	Urban	Rural	Total	Urban	Rural
Coefficients by lag									
0	−0.15	−0.39	0.03	0.04	0.03	0.04	0.23**	0.22	0.24*
1	−0.27	0.33	−0.67	−0.22	−0.22	−0.22	−0.08	−0.13	−0.04
2	0.83**	0.27	1.17**	0.25	0.19	0.29**	0.15	0.08	0.19
Sum of coefficients	0.41	0.21	0.53	0.07	0.00	0.11	0.31	0.17	0.39
Tests (p-values)[a]									
Coefficients are zero	.00**	.44	.00**	.17	.79	.18	.00**	.19	.00**
Sum of coefficients is zero	.00**	.28	.00**	.31	.98	.20	.00**	.11	.00**

NOTES: Age of woman, interval since first birth, and year are controlled.   GDP, real gross domestic product per capita, 1964-1988; EXQ, export quantum index, 1964-1988; TT, terms of trade index, 1964-1988; WPCOC, real world price of cocoa, 1964-1987; WPOIL, real world price of crude petroleum, 1964-1987; PPCOC, real producer price of cocoa, 1964-1988.

[a] * indicates a p-value of < .10; ** means a p-value of < .05.

WPCOC			WPOIL			PPCOC		
Total	Urban	Rural	Total	Urban	Rural	Total	Urban	Rural
0.14	−0.14	0.30**	0.25**	0.24**	0.26**	−0.53**	−0.56**	−0.53**
−0.16	0.28	−0.41**	−0.07	−0.17	−0.01	0.34**	0.58**	0.22
0.20**	0.10	0.26**	0.19*	0.25	0.14	−0.11	−0.44**	0.07
0.17	0.24	0.14	0.37	0.33	0.39	−0.30	−0.42	−0.24
.11	.05**	.03**	.00**	.05**	.00**	.00**	.01**	.00**
.03**	.07*	.15	.00**	.02**	.00**	.01**	.04**	.10

SENEGAL

Economic Experience

The World Bank (1989b) lists Senegal as a lower-middle-income country, whose GNP per capita was $520 in 1987. Agriculture accounted for 22 percent of output in 1987, and industry's share was 27 percent. In 1980, 81 percent of the labor force worked in agriculture. The primary agricultural products are groundnuts, millet, sorghum, maize, manioc, rice, and livestock. In the late 1980s, about 40 percent of total cultivated land was in groundnuts, which are largely exported (Central Intelligence Agency, 1989). Other major exports include phosphates and fish. Senegal imports crude petroleum and exports refined petroleum products.

The Senegalese economy has been stagnant for the past three decades, as Figure 5-11 shows. There was some growth in the early 1960s, followed by a decline from 1968 through 1974, a brief period of expansion in the mid-1970s, and subsequent erratic growth. Senegal's inability to sustain growth has been attributed to several factors. The first is rainfall. Rainfall in Senegal is extremely variable, and droughts are frequent. Yields of millet, rice, and groundnuts are quite sensitive to fluctuations in rainfall (Gersovitz, 1987). Furthermore, rainfall is low enough on average to prevent farmers from making wide use of fertilizer-intensive farming techniques. Second, the Senegalese economy (and government revenues) is dependent on export earnings from phosphates. However, phosphate deposits have been heavily mined and are of increasingly inferior quality (World Bank, 1991).

The prices of exports, particularly of groundnuts and phosphates, are a major determinant of income in Senegal. Both of these commodities experienced a short-lived boom in the 1970s (leading to a brief period of growth) but have subsequently collapsed. The Senegalese government stabilizes prices for many agricultural outputs, including groundnuts. These policies are meant to buffer farmers against short-term fluctuations in world prices; however, over the long run, the producer prices move with world prices. Groundnut farmers have experienced nearly continuous declines in the price of their output since the boom in 1974.

In what follows, we investigate the relationship between demographic outcomes and several economic indicators. These include per capita GDP, the terms of trade and quantity of exports, the world prices of phosphates and groundnuts, the producer price of groundnuts, and rainfall. Real per capita GDP serves as a general economic indicator, which should affect demographic outcomes in both rural and urban areas. The terms of trade and export quantities also serve as general economic indicators. Movements in the world prices of phosphates and groundnuts should have a large effect on government revenues and might be expected to have larger effects in urban than in rural areas. The producer price of groundnuts and the rainfall measure serve as proxies for rural living standards, and we expect the effects of these variables to be larger in rural areas.

Demographic Outcomes

After a plateau in the 1960s and early 1970s, child mortality has fallen sharply (Hill, 1993). Fertility remains high—6.6 children per woman in 1986; but fertility may be falling among younger age groups (Cohen, 1993), and the age of marriage is increasing, if only slightly (van de Walle, 1993).

Figure 5-11 and Table 5-18 show the strong downward trend in mortality from 1970 to 1985 for the total and rural samples. However, there has been no significant variation around the trend. Not surprisingly, the effects of economic variables on variation net of trend in mortality are mixed (Table 5-19). For the sample of rural children, the current and lagged values of the quantity of exports as a group have an effect on mortality. The effect of the current value is in the expected negative direction, but the sum of coefficients is not significantly different from zero. Also for the rural sample, the sums of the coefficients on the terms of trade and on rainfall (RAIN) are significantly greater than zero, that is, increases in these indicators are associated with increases in infant and child mortality, perverse results.[15]

For the urban sample, the sums of the coefficients for two of the economic variables, terms of trade and the world price of groundnuts, are negative and relatively large. That the latter is significantly different from zero for urban areas is consistent with the expectation stated above that changes in world prices will affect government revenues and thus urban populations relatively more than rural ones.

The log of odds of marriage in Senegal declined from 1960 to 1985 for all three samples, especially the urban population (Table 5-18 and Figures 5-11, 5-12, and 5-13), but there was no significant variation around the trend. Three of the economic variables had the hypothesized positive effects on marriage for the total sample: the terms of trade, the world price of groundnuts, and the producer price of groundnuts (see Table 5-20). The first two also had significant positive effects on the log odds for the urban sample. For the rural sample, only the terms of trade had significant effects, which were positive in sum.

The log odds of first birth also fell over time in the total and urban samples, but rose in the rural one, as was the case in Nigeria.[16] There was

---

[15]The positive relation between mortality and rainfall is perverse from an economic perspective, but from an epidemiological one, it is not implausible, given that the transmission of some diseases, such as malaria, is positively associated with rainfall.

[16]However, for the total sample, there was no significant trend once education was controlled for ($p = .82$).

significant variation around the trend for the total and rural samples. For the total sample, the terms of trade and the world and producer prices of groundnuts all had significantly positive effects in sum (Table 5-21). For the urban sample, the terms of trade and the world price of phosphates also had positive effects, and those for the former were large. The coefficients on the economic variables as a group and in sum were not significantly different from zero in the analysis of the rural sample.[17]

There was a significant downward trend in the log odds of second birth for all three samples and significant variation net of the trend for the total and the rural samples (Table 5-18).[18] The results in Table 5-22 indicate that for the total sample, the terms of trade and the world price of groundnuts had the hypothesized positive effects. For the urban sample, the world prices of groundnuts and phosphates and the producer price of groundnuts all had positive effects, but GDP and RAIN had negative effects, those for the former being quite strong. For the rural sample, the quantity of exports also had a negative effect, whereas the terms of trade, the world price of groundnuts, and rain had positive effects.[19]

In summary, the results for Senegal for mortality and second births are quite mixed and do not give a strong impression that economic factors have had demographic effects; but the results are consistent with the hypothesis that economic upturns have had positive effects on marriages and first births net of trends. However, one economic indicator, the world price of groundnuts, does have the hypothesized effects across all the outcomes, a finding that is consistent with the importance of groundnuts in the Senegalese economy, at the time. These effects tend to be most frequent and greatest for the urban sample, which is consistent with the role of government in stabilizing prices to producers in the short run and absorbing shocks via government expenditures. That some of the other broad indicators of the economy, such as GDP, do not have such consistent effects may reflect the relatively undramatic changes in these indicators in recent decades.

---

[17]There were also two changes in the economic effects when education was added to the model: GDP as a group, urban ($p = .10$), but the sum is negative; and WPGN in sum (positive), urban ($p = .06$).

[18]The trend was not significant ($p = .11$) for the rural sample when education was controlled for.

[19]The sum of the coefficients on EXQ were also significantly negative in the model including education for the total sample ($p = .09$).

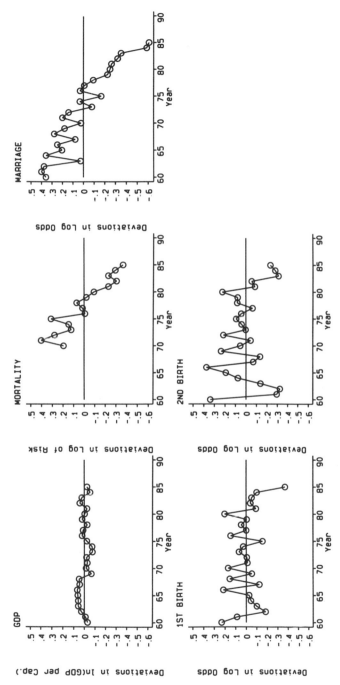

FIGURE 5-11 Time pattern of deviations in the logarithm of real gross domestic product per capita and the estimated demographic outcomes, total sample, Senegal.

TABLE 5-18   Effects of Time Period on Demographic Outcomes, Senegal

	Child Mortality[a]			First Marriage[b]		
	Total	Urban	Rural	Total	Urban	Rural
Trend	−.05	−.00	−.06	−.04	−.06	−.02
Tests (p-values)[c]						
No trend	.00**	.86	.00**	.00**	.00**	.00**
No variation	.00**	.25	.00**	.00**	.00**	.03**
No variation net of trend	.35	.21	.26	.27	.70	.69
Number						
Children	14,225	3,365	7,172	—	—	—
Women	—	—	—	4,407	1,403	2,977

[a]In mortality analysis, age of child is controlled. Period of analysis is 1970-1985.

[b]In marriage and first-birth analyses age of woman is controlled; in second-birth analysis, age of woman and interval since first birth are controlled. Period of analysis is 1960-1985.

[c] * indicates a p-value of < .10; ** means a p-value of < .05.

First Birth[b]			Second Birth[b]		
Total	Urban	Rural	Total	Urban	Rural
−.01	−.03	.01	−.01	−.02	−.01
.02**	.00**	.03**	.01**	.03**	.07*
.00**	.00**	.03**	.01**	.08*	.02**
.02**	.56	.06*	.04**	.17	.03**
—	—	—	—	—	—
4,407	1,430	2,977	3,242	870	2,312

TABLE 5-19 Effects of Economic Variables on Child Mortality, Senegal

	GDP			EXQ			TT			WPGN		
	Total	Urban	Rural	Total	Urban	Rural	Total	Urban	Rural	Total	Urban	Rural
Coefficients by lag												
0	-0.55	-2.65	-0.39	-0.11	0.41	-0.39**	0.21	0.19	0.15	-0.06	-0.49	0.06
1	0.14	0.99	0.76	0.12	0.52	0.03	0.15	-0.49	0.27	0.21**	0.11	0.09
2	-1.11*	0.49	-0.23	0.07	-0.13	0.27	-0.11	-0.95*	0.07	-0.03	-0.48*	0.04
Sum of coefficients	-1.53	-1.17	0.14	0.08	0.80	-0.09	0.25	-1.25	0.49	0.13	-0.85	0.19
Tests (p-values)[a]												
Coefficients are zero	.39	.43	.83	.63	.38	.07*	.42	.07*	.34	.18	.04**	.64
Sum of coefficients is zero	.21	.75	.89	.74	.22	.76	.24	.06*	.08*	.26	.01**	.21

continued

TABLE 5-19 Continued

	WPPH			PPGN			RAIN		
	Total	Urban	Rural	Total	Urban	Rural	Total	Urban	Rural
Coefficients by lag									
0	0.02	-0.09	-0.05	-0.14	-1.26**	-0.11	0.21	-0.27	0.41**
1	0.07	0.11	0.05	0.38**	0.85	0.04	0.09	0.05	0.15
2	-0.07	-0.19	-0.04	-0.21	-0.59	-0.04	0.05	-0.20	0.16
Sum of coefficients	0.02	-0.19	-0.05	0.03	-1.00	-0.11	0.34	-0.42	0.72
Tests (p-values)[a]									
Coefficients are zero	.53	.86	.97	.26	.21	.97	.40	.90	.13
Sum of coefficients is zero	.81	.49	.70	.87	.16	.72	.21	.53	.04**

NOTES: Age of child and year are controlled. GDP, real gross domestic product per capita, 1970-1985; EXQ, export quantum index, 1970-1985; TT, terms of trade index, 1970-1985; WPGN, real world price of ground nuts, 1970-1985; WPPH, real world price of phosphates, 1970-1985; PPGN, real producer price of ground nuts, 1970-1985; RAIN, rainfall, July-September, Diourbel, 1970-1980.

[a] * indicates a p-value of < .10; ** means a p-value of < .05.

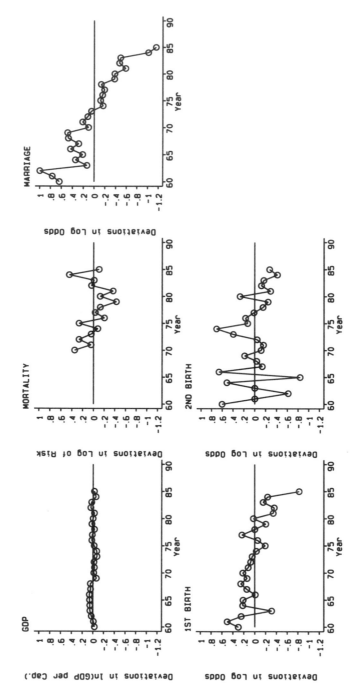

FIGURE 5-12 Time pattern of deviations in the logarithm of real gross domestic product per capita and the estimated demographic outcomes, urban sample, Senegal.

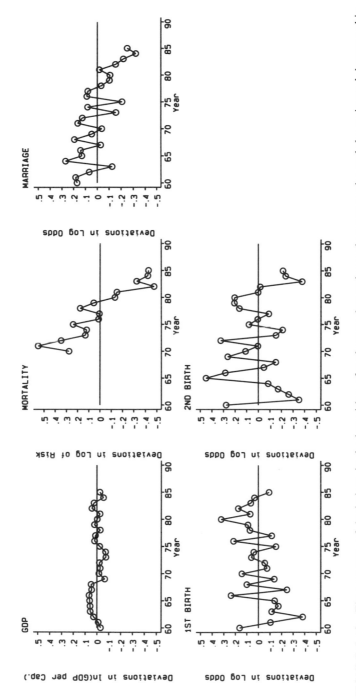

FIGURE 5-13   Time pattern of deviations in the logarithm of real gross domestic product per capita and the estimated demographic outcomes, rural sample, Senegal.

TABLE 5-20 Effects of Economic Variables on Marriage, Senegal

	GDP			EXQ			TT			WPGN		
	Total	Urban	Rural	Total	Urban	Rural	Total	Urban	Rural	Total	Urban	Rural
Coefficients by lag												
0	-0.02	-0.23	0.24	-0.03	-0.08	-0.05	0.23	-0.30	0.32	0.14	-0.05	0.18
1	0.50	1.37	0.21	-0.10	-0.02	-0.18	0.05	0.57	-0.16	-0.06	0.12	-0.14
2	-1.09**	-1.89*	-0.38	0.02	-0.37	0.18	0.33*	0.33	0.31	0.18*	0.24	0.12
Sum of coefficients	-0.61	-0.75	0.07	-0.11	-0.48	-0.05	0.61	0.60	0.47	0.26	0.31	0.16
Tests (p-values)[a]												
Coefficients are zero	.27	.32	.91	.90	.49	.48	.02**	.15	.20	.03**	.23	.27
Sum of coefficients is zero	.38	.57	.94	.65	.30	.86	.00**	.10*	.05**	.01**	.08*	.16

continued

TABLE 5-20 *Continued*

	WPPH			PPGN			RAIN		
	Total	Urban	Rural	Total	Urban	Rural	Total	Urban	Rural
Coefficients by lag									
0	0.07	−0.09	0.09	0.21	−0.24	0.35*	0.07	0.11	0.07
1	−0.08	0.07	−0.13	0.04	0.64*	−0.24	0.01	−0.00	0.03
2	0.16*	0.06	0.18*	0.17	−0.06	0.19	0.16	0.25	0.15
Sum of coefficients	0.15	0.04	0.14	0.41	0.35	0.29	0.23	0.36	0.25
Tests (p-values)[a]									
Coefficients are zero	.24	.79	.35	.26	.25	.38	.49	.63	.71
Sum of coefficients is zero	.11	.82	.21	.05*	.39	.25	.37	.47	.41

NOTES: Age of woman and year are controlled. GDP, real gross domestic product per capita, 1960-1985; EXQ, export quantum index, 1960-1985; TT, terms of trade index, 1960-1985; WPGN, real world price of ground nuts, 1960-1985; WPPH, real world price of phosphates, 1960-1985; PPGN, real producer price of ground nuts, 1960-1985; RAIN, rainfall, July-September, Diourbel, 1960-1980.

[a] * indicates a *p*-value of < .10; ** means a *p*-value of < .05.

TABLE 5-21 Effects of Economic Variables on First Births, Senegal

	GDP			EXQ			TT			WPGN		
	Total	Urban	Rural	Total	Urban	Rural	Total	Urban	Rural	Total	Urban	Rural
Coefficients by lag												
0	0.05	-1.23	0.69	-0.06	-0.03	-0.07	-0.12	0.39	-0.41	0.03	0.18	-0.07
1	0.69	2.70**	-0.06	-0.02	0.34	-0.18	0.04	-0.50	0.21	-0.06	-0.16	-0.03
2	-0.64	-1.71	-0.00	-0.13	-0.21	-0.13	0.50**	0.92**	0.28	0.25**	0.26	0.23**
Sum of coefficients	0.10	-0.23	0.64	-0.21	0.10	-0.38	0.42	0.81	0.09	0.23	0.27	0.13
Tests (p-values)[a]												
Coefficients are zero	.55	.10	.75	.75	.48	.60	.02**	.04**	.17	.02**	.29	.20
Sum of coefficients is zero	.89	.86	.44	.39	.82	.20	.03**	.02**	.71	.01**	.11	.25

continued

TABLE 5-21 *Continued*

	WPPH			PPGN			RAIN		
	Total	Urban	Rural	Total	Urban	Rural	Total	Urban	Rural
Coefficients by lag									
0	0.08	0.17	0.02	0.09	-0.08	0.12	-0.08	-0.10	-0.07
1	-0.13	-0.35*	-0.04	-0.04	0.07	-0.10	0.06	-0.07	0.13
2	0.16*	0.41**	0.05	0.30*	0.51	0.17	0.13	0.09	0.16
Sum of coefficients	0.11	0.22	0.03	0.35	0.49	0.19	0.11	-0.09	0.22
Tests (p-values)[a]									
Coefficients are zero	.31	.09*	.97	.30	.31	.85	.31	.84	.31
Sum of coefficients is zero	.24	.21	.78	.09*	.22	.45	.69	.86	.47

NOTES: Age of woman and year are controlled. GDP, real gross domestic product per capita, 1960-1985; EXQ, export quantum index, 1960-1985; TT, terms of trade index, 1960-1985; WPGN, real world price of ground nuts, 1960-1985; WPPH, real world price of phosphates, 1960-1985; PPGN, real producer price of ground nuts, 1960-1985; RAIN, rainfall, July-September, Diourbel, 1960-1980.

[a] * indicates a *p*-value of < .10; ** means a *p*-value of < .05.

TABLE 5-22 Effects of Economic Variables on Second Births, Senegal

	GDP			EXQ			TT			WPGN		
	Total	Urban	Rural	Total	Urban	Rural	Total	Urban	Rural	Total	Urban	Rural
Coefficients by lag												
0	-0.29	-1.66	0.22	-0.30	0.24	-0.50**	0.15	0.48	-0.02	-0.01	0.31	-0.14
1	-0.31	0.20	-0.56	-0.25	0.32	-0.48**	0.29	-0.66	0.64*	0.29**	0.06	0.37**
2	-0.25	-2.67*	0.63	0.02	-0.35	0.15	0.18	0.68	0.01	0.06	0.18	0.01
Sum of coefficients	-0.86	-4.13	0.29	-0.53	0.21	-0.83	0.62	0.50	0.63	0.33	0.55	0.24
Tests (p-values)a Coefficients are zero	.85	.16	.89	.26	.53	.02**	.10	.46	.08*	.02**	.15	.07*
Sum of coefficients is zero	.38	.03**	.80	.10	.74	.03**	.02**	.33	.04**	.01**	.02**	.09*

continued

TABLE 5-22 Continued

	WPPH			PPGN			RAIN		
	Total	Urban	Rural	Total	Urban	Rural	Total	Urban	Rural
Coefficients by lag									
0	0.06	0.62**	-0.15	-0.05	0.55	-0.27	0.19	-0.26	0.36*
1	0.03	-0.40	0.20	0.24	0.05	0.34	0.12	-0.72**	0.41**
2	-0.07	0.15	-0.17	-0.18	0.35	-0.39	0.17	0.09	0.22
Sum of coefficients	0.02	0.37	-0.12	0.02	0.95	-0.32	0.48	-0.89	1.00
Tests (p-values)[a]									
Coefficients are zero	.69	.05*	.60	.75	.38	.52	.62	.06*	.09*
Sum of coefficients is zero	.88	.15	.42	.95	.09*	.34	.20	.22	.02**

NOTES: Age of woman, interval since first birth, and year are controlled. GDP, real gross domestic product per capita, 1960-1985; EXQ, export quantum index, 1960-1985; TT, terms of trade index, 1960-1985; WPGN, real world price of ground nuts, 1960-1985; WPPH, real world price of phosphates, 1960-1985; PPGN, real producer price of ground nuts, 1960-1985; RAIN, rainfall, July-September, Diourbel, 1960-1980.

[a] * indicates a p-value of < .10; ** means a p-value of < .05.

TOGO

Economic Experience

Togo is listed by the World Bank (1989b) as a lower-income country; its GNP per capita was $290 in 1987. Agriculture accounted for 29 percent of GDP in 1987, and employed 73 percent of the labor force in 1980. The share of GDP from industry was 18 percent in 1987. The major food crops are yams, cassava, maize, beans, rice, millet, sorghum, and fish. Export crops include coffee, cocoa, and cotton. Phosphates are an important export, accounting for around 50 percent of total export earnings in the early 1980s. Government revenue is also heavily dependent on phosphate exports, because of government ownership of phosphate mines (World Bank, 1991).

As Figure 5-14 illustrates, per capita output in Togo grew through the 1960s and 1970s, and then declined in the 1980s. Through the 1960s, phosphate mining was an increasingly large source of incomes and government revenues. Between 1973 and 1975, the real price of phosphates more than tripled. The prices of coffee and cocoa, two other important exports, experienced booms in 1977. The increase in government revenues due to these price increases was used to finance an ambitious investment program, to which 46 percent of GDP was allocated in 1978. However, the collapse in the prices of export goods after 1978 resulted in debt problems. External public debt rose from 16 percent of GNP in 1970 to 82 percent in 1980.

After 1983, Togo began a series of stabilization policies aimed at increasing exports and reducing debt burdens. It increased producer prices for major export crops (cocoa, coffee, and cotton) and privatized several public enterprises (World Bank, 1991). However, continued adverse movements in its terms of trade and declines in phosphate exports combined to yield slow or negative growth in the years between 1983 and 1988. By 1988, real producer prices for coffee and cocoa had fallen below those of 1980, suggesting declines in rural living standards. However, the government increased expenditures on education, health, and social services between 1980 and 1987, a period over which per capita incomes fell (World Bank, 1989b).

Indirect evidence suggests that neither the commodity price boom in the 1970s nor its collapse in the 1980s affected the incomes of rural households very much. Togo maintains stable producer prices for coffee and cocoa despite fluctuations in world prices. Evidence of this policy comes directly from the series on producer and world prices reported in appendix Tables A-6 and A-8. The coefficients of variation of the world prices of coffee and cocoa over the 1960-1987 period were both 39 percent. The coefficients of variation of producer prices of coffee and cocoa were 19

percent and 20 percent, respectively. When the world prices of these commodities experienced large increases in the 1970s, producer prices rose only
slightly. Likewise, declines in commodity prices were not matched by large
declines in producer prices. Moreover, coffee and cocoa production is concentrated in the plateau region. Even so, households throughout the country
may have been indirectly affected by the commodity price movements via
changes in government expenditures.

Some evidence points to a drought and famine centered on 1977, which
is not reflected in the time series of GDP per capita and may have been
important for certain segments of the population. The per capita production
of cereals was 15 percent lower in 1977 than it was in 1976 (Food and
Agriculture Organization, 1983). In our analysis, we have also not captured
potential influences in Togo of the economic shock in neighboring Nigeria
delivered by the fall in oil prices.

In what follows, we examine whether demographic outcomes have been
affected by movements in per capita GDP, the terms of trade, export quantities, the world prices of phosphates, coffee, and cocoa, and producer prices
of coffee and cocoa. As it does for other countries, per capita GDP serves
as a general indicator of living standards. Indirect evidence suggests that
the terms of trade and world prices of commodities may be more important
determinants of living standards in urban than in rural areas. The producer
prices serve as measures of rural living standards.

Demographic Outcomes

Child mortality declined steadily from 1960 to 1985 and was halved
over the period (Hill, 1993). Fertility, however, remains high—the total
fertility rate is over six (Cohen, 1993); and the age of marriage has remained virtually constant (van de Walle, 1993).

The downward trend in mortality from 1970 to 1987 for the total and
rural samples is shown in Figures 5-14 and 5-16 and Table 5-23. There is
no significant trend for urban children, and there was no significant variation around the trend for any of the groups.

The effects of economic variables on mortality are mixed (Table 5-24).
For the total sample, the quantity of exports and the producer prices of
cocoa and coffee are all negatively related to child mortality net of trend, as
hypothesized, but the world price of phosphates (WPPH) has a positive
effect. For the urban sample, only the coefficients on the world price of
coffee as a group are significantly different from zero. For the rural sample,
the sum of the coefficients on EXQ is significantly less than zero, but
WPCOC and WPPH have positive effects.

There was a downward trend in the log odds of marriage for all three
samples from 1963 to 1988 (Figures 5-14, 5-15, and 5-16 and Table 5-23),

but there was no significant variation around the trends.[20]   As shown in Table 5-25, the economic effects net of trend are strongest for the urban sample: GDP, TT, WPCOC, and WPPH all had positive effects.[21]   The effects of GDP, TT, and PPCOC are also positive for the total sample.   The coefficients on the economic variables for the rural models are not significantly different from zero either as a group or in sum.

There was a significant downward trend in the log odds of first birth for the total and urban samples, for which there was also significant variation around the trend (Table 5-23).[22]   However, only TT and WPPH had significant effects, which were positive in sum, for the total and urban samples (Table 5-26).[23]

The log odds of second birth show significant trends downward for all three samples, but without significant variation net of the trends (Table 5-23); and the economic variables had no effects (Table 5-27).

In summary, the effects of economic factors net of trend on mortality are mixed in Togo.   The effects on marriage for urban women are consistently positive, and first births show a few effects for the total and urban samples.   There are no effects on second births.   Economic reversals thus appear to have affected primarily marriage and first births, especially in urban areas.   The world price of Togo's most important commodity, phosphates, and the terms of trade affected both outcomes.

---

[20]These trends become insignificant once education is entered into the models ($p = .99$ for total, $p = .25$ for urban, and $p = .43$ for rural).

[21]The effects of WPCOC and WPPH become insignificant when education is controlled for (p-values for both are .13).

[22]The trends are insignificant for models with education ($p = .95$ for total and $p = .30$ for urban).

[23]The effects of TT as a group are not significant for the urban model with education ($p = .11$).

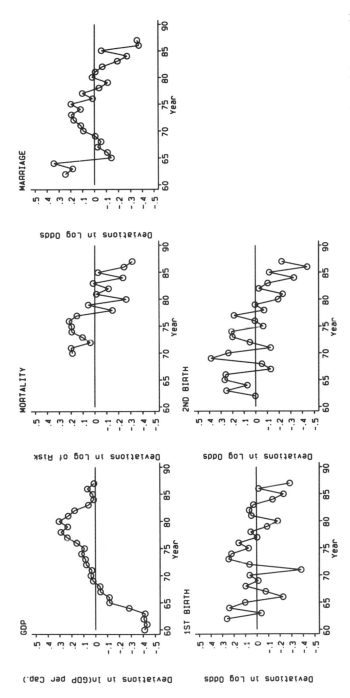

FIGURE 5-14 Time pattern of deviations in the logarithm of real gross domestic product per capita and the estimated demographic outcomes, total sample, Togo.

TABLE 5-23   Effects of Time Period on Demographic Outcomes, Togo

	Child Mortality[a]			First Marriage[b]		
	Total	Urban	Rural	Total	Urban	Rural
Trend	−.03	−.00	−.03	−.02	−.02	−.01
Tests (p-values)[c]						
No trend	.00**	.82	.00**	.00**	.00**	.00**
No variation	.00**	.38	.01**	.00**	.00**	.03**
No variation						
net of trend	.42	.32	.11	.17	.12	.16*
Number						
Children	10,782	1,704	5,439	—	—	—
Women	—	—	—	3,355	1,261	2,094

[a]In mortality analysis, age of child is controlled. Period of analysis is 1970-1985.

[b]In marriage and first-birth analyses, age of woman is controlled; in second-birth analysis, age of woman and interval since first birth are controlled. Period of analysis is 1960-1985.

[c] * indicates a p-value of < .10; ** means a p-value of < .05.

First Birth[b]			Second Birth[b]		
Total	Urban	Rural	Total	Urban	Rural
−.01	−.02	−.00	−.02	−.02	−.02
.00**	.00**	.32	.00**	.00**	.00**
.01**	.01**	.11	.01**	.29	.08*
.04**	.05*	.11	.59	.74	.53
—	—	—	—	—	—
3,355	1,261	2,094	2,472	864	1,608

TABLE 5-24 Effects of Economic Variables on Child Mortality, Togo

	GDP			EXQ			TT			WPCOC		
	Total	Urban	Rural	Total	Urban	Rural	Total	Urban	Rural	Total	Urban	Rural
Coefficients by lag												
0	-0.66	0.39	-0.18	-0.32**	0.14	-0.38*	0.03	-0.81	0.40	0.19*	0.23	0.34**
1	0.66	0.95	1.09	0.00	0.12	0.13	0.34	-0.29	0.05	-0.22	0.07	-0.23
2	-0.17	-0.80	-0.41	-0.11	-0.67	-0.30	-0.19	0.97	0.20	0.06	-0.01	0.21
Sum of coefficients	-0.17	0.54	0.51	-0.43	-0.40	-0.56	0.18	-0.13	0.65	0.03	0.29	0.31
Tests (p-values)[a]												
Coefficients are zero	.65	.86	.44	.06*	.37	.18	.14	.21	.04**	.37	.80	.15
Sum of coefficients is zero	.57	.58	.23	.02**	.52	.04**	.24	.81	.01**	.75	.43	.04**

continued

TABLE 24-Continued

	WPCOF			WPPH			PPCOC			PPCOF		
	Total	Urban	Rural	Total	Urban	Rural	Total	Urban	Rural	Total	Urban	Rural
Coefficients by lag												
0	0.17	-0.07	0.21	0.08	-0.37	0.25	-0.33	0.05	0.22	-0.37	-0.35	0.20
1	-0.21	0.91**	-0.10	0.08	-0.28	-0.03	-0.10	0.21	-0.53*	-0.22	-0.15	-0.60
2	-0.01	-0.51	0.08	0.06	0.52	0.24	-0.13	-0.30	-0.00	-0.20	-0.31	-0.04
Sum of coefficients	-0.05	0.33	0.18	0.21	-0.13	0.47	-0.57	-0.04	-0.31	-0.79	-0.82	-0.44
Tests (p-values)[a]												
Coefficients are zero	.22	.08*	.55	.20	.24	.04**	.25	.97	.39	.31	.95	.42
Sum of coefficients is zero	.65	.41	.27	.06*	.74	.00**	.05*	.96	.47	.06*	.57	.49

NOTES: Age of child and year are controlled. GDP, real gross domestic product per capita, 1970-1988; EXQ, export quantum index, 1970-1988; TT, terms of trade index, 1970-1988; WPCOC, real world price of cocoa, 1970-1987; WPCOF, real world price of coffee, 1970-1987; WPPH, real world price of phosphates, 1970-1987; PPCOC, real producer price of cocoa, 1970-1987; PPCOF, real producer price of coffee, 1970-1987.

[a] * indicates a p-value of $< .10$; ** means a p-value of $< .05$.

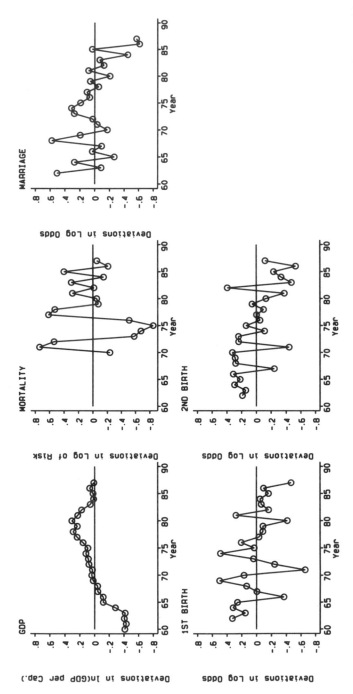

FIGURE 5-15 Time pattern of deviations in the logarithm of real gross domestic product per capita and the estimated demographic outcomes, urban sample, Togo.

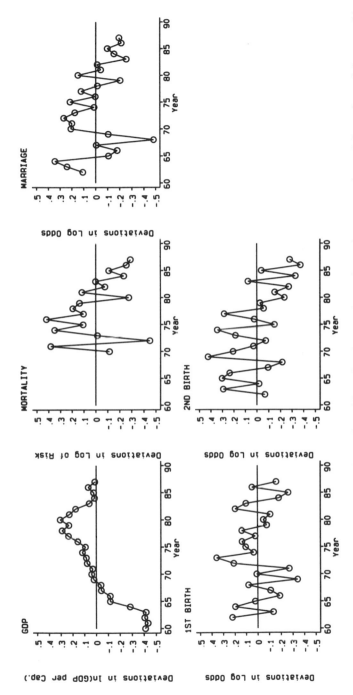

FIGURE 5-16 Time pattern of deviations in the logarithm of real gross domestic product per capita and the estimated demographic outcomes, rural sample, Togo.

TABLE 5-25 Effects of Economic Variables on Marriage, Togo

	GDP			EXQ			TT			WPCOC		
	Total	Urban	Rural	Total	Urban	Rural	Total	Urban	Rural	Total	Urban	Rural
Coefficients by lag												
0	0.28	-0.64	0.79	-0.11	-0.25	-0.02	0.22	0.36	0.14	0.06	0.37**	-0.11
1	-0.59	0.92	-1.38*	0.02	0.11	-0.04	0.08	0.02	0.11	0.06	-0.17	0.18
2	0.75*	0.41	0.91*	0.10	0.02	0.14	-0.00	0.04	-0.03	0.01	0.08	-0.02
Sum of coefficients	0.45	0.69	0.33	0.01	-0.11	0.08	0.29	0.42	0.22	0.14	0.28	0.05
Tests (p-values)[a]												
Coefficients are zero	.06*	.09*	.13	.58	.62	.78	.05*	.12	.41	.39	.09*	.62
Sum of coefficients is zero	.01**	.03**	.15	.96	.66	.65	.02**	.04**	.16	.13	.06*	.66

continued

TABLE 5-25 *Continued*

	WPCOF			WPPH			PPCOC			PPCOF		
	Total	Urban	Rural	Total	Urban	Rural	Total	Urban	Rural	Total	Urban	Rural
Coefficients by lag												
0	0.07	0.11	0.03	0.13	0.29*	0.04	-0.07	0.05	-0.14	-0.28**	-0.11	-0.38**
1	0.03	-0.08	0.09	0.03	-0.05	0.07	0.22*	0.27	0.19	0.01	0.15	-0.07
2	-0.03	0.14	-0.13	-0.03	0.06	-0.09	0.13	-0.07	0.24*	-0.02	-0.20	0.08
Sum of coefficients	0.06	0.17	-0.01	0.13	0.30	0.02	0.28	0.25	0.30	-0.29	-0.15	-0.38
Tests (p-values)[a]												
Coefficients are zero	.78	.76	.68	.18	.14	.70	.09*	.53	.10	.22	.71	.15
Sum of coefficients is zero	.55	.34	.97	.22	.08*	.88	.06*	.32	.11	.16	.65	.14

NOTES: Age of woman and year are controlled. GDP, real gross domestic product per capita, 1963-1988; EXQ, export quantum index, 1963-1988; TT, terms of trade index, 1963-1988; WPCOC, real world price of cocoa, 1963-1987; WPCOF, real world price of coffee, 1963-1987; WPPH, real world price of phosphates, 1963-1987; PPCOC, real producer price of cocoa, 1963-1987; PPCOF, real producer price of coffee, 1963-1987.

[a] * indicates a p-value of < .10; ** means a p-value of < .05.

TABLE 5-26 Effects of Economic Variables on First Births, Togo

	GDP			EXQ			TT			WPCOC		
	Total	Urban	Rural	Total	Urban	Rural	Total	Urban	Rural	Total	Urban	Rural
Coefficients by lag												
0	0.25	0.03	0.35	-0.16	-0.33	-0.08	0.24*	0.52**	0.06	0.11	0.15	0.08
1	-0.39	-0.15	-0.52	-0.08	0.11	-0.19	-0.12	-0.20	-0.07	-0.01	0.11	-0.08
2	0.38	0.26	0.45	0.03	-0.17	0.13	0.13	-0.10	0.25	-0.07	-0.20	-0.00
Sum of coefficients	0.24	0.13	0.29	-0.22	-0.39	-0.14	0.25	0.23	0.25	0.03	0.06	0.00
Tests (p-values)[a]												
Coefficients are zero	.53	.97	.55	.26	.36	.43	.16	.09*	.36	.46	.26	.92
Sum of coefficients is zero	.18	.67	.21	.14	.12	.46	.04**	.28	.11	.76	.69	.97

continued

TABLE 5-26 *Continued*

	WPCOF			WPPH			PPCOC			PPCOF		
	Total	Urban	Rural	Total	Urban	Rural	Total	Urban	Rural	Total	Urban	Rural
Coefficients by lag												
0	0.13	0.12	0.14	0.18*	0.43**	0.01	0.13	0.16	0.11	0.16	0.21	0.13
1	-0.20	-0.26	-0.17	-0.04	-0.19	0.08	-0.15	-0.11	-0.17	-0.30**	-0.18	-0.36**
2	0.07	0.07	0.07	0.08	0.16	0.02	0.17	0.18	0.16	0.03	0.20	-0.07
Sum of coefficients	0.00	-0.07	0.03	0.22	0.40	0.11	0.16	0.23	0.11	-0.11	0.23	-0.31
Tests (p-values)[a]												
Coefficients are zero	.43	.67	.70	.13	.02**	.79	.26	.63	.49	.14	.56	.16
Sum of coefficients is zero	.99	.69	.80	.03**	.02**	.41	.30	.35	.57	.58	.51	.23

NOTES: Age of woman and year are controlled. GDP, real gross domestic product per capita, 1963-1988; EXQ, export quantum index, 1963-1988; TT, terms of trade index, 1963-1988; WPCOC, real world price of cocoa, 1963-1987; WPCOF, real world price of coffee, 1963-1987; WPPH, real world price of phosphates, 1963-1987; PPCOC, real producer price of cocoa, 1963-1987; PPCOF, real producer price of coffee, 1963-1987.

[a] * indicates a *p*-value of < .10; ** means a *p*-value of < .05.

TABLE 5-27 Effects of Economic Variables on Second Births, Togo

	GDP			EXQ			TT			WPCOC		
	Total	Urban	Rural	Total	Urban	Rural	Total	Urban	Rural	Total	Urban	Rural
Coefficients by lag												
0	0.09	−0.20	0.20	0.15	0.24	0.10	0.12	−0.17	0.26	0.26*	0.04	0.35**
1	0.41	0.40	0.48	−0.19	−0.25	−0.14	−0.16	0.07	−0.28	−0.15	−0.09	−0.15
2	−0.23	0.11	−0.46	0.08	0.37	−0.09	0.23	0.15	0.25	0.01	0.11	−0.04
Sum of coefficients	0.27	0.31	0.22	0.03	0.36	−0.13	0.19	0.05	0.23	0.13	0.06	0.15
Tests (p-values)[a]												
Coefficients are zero	.63	.87	.74	.75	.56	.74	.59	.90	.55	.21	.98	.11
Sum of coefficients is zero	.26	.45	.47	.87	.30	.61	.25	.85	.25	.30	.77	.33

continued

TABLE 5-27 Continued

	WPCOF			WPPH			PPCOC			PPCOF		
	Total	Urban	Rural	Total	Urban	Rural	Total	Urban	Rural	Total	Urban	Rural
Coefficients by lag												
0	0.12	0.02	0.15	0.13	-0.17	0.27	-0.05	-0.04	-0.08	-0.02	-0.01	-0.04
1	-0.01	-0.21	0.11	-0.17	0.24	-0.36*	0.15	0.23	0.12	0.09	0.22	0.03
2	-0.02	0.24	-0.18	0.19	-0.13	0.33**	-0.10	-0.05	-0.11	-0.31*	-0.19	-0.37*
Sum of coefficients	0.09	0.05	0.08	0.15	-0.06	0.24	-0.00	0.14	-0.07	-0.24	0.01	-0.38
Tests (p-values)[a]												
Coefficients are zero	.73	.72	.35	.54	.88	.20	.76	.86	.87	.30	.83	.35
Sum of coefficients is zero	.52	.81	.63	.27	.79	.16	1.00	.66	.75	.35	.98	.24

NOTES: Age of woman, interval since first birth, and year are controlled. GDP, real gross domestic product per capita, 1963-1988; EXQ, export quantum index, 1963-1988; TT, terms of trade index, 1963-1988; WPCOC, real world price of cocoa, 1963-1987; WPCOF, real world price of coffee, 1963-1987; WPPH, real world price of phosphates, 1963-1987; PPCOC, real producer price of cocoa, 1963-1987; PPCOF, real producer price of coffee, 1963-1987.

[a] * indicates a *p*-value of < .10; ** means a *p*-value of < .05.

UGANDA

Economic Experience

With a GNP per capita of $260 in 1987, Uganda is the poorest country considered in our study (World Bank, 1989b). Unlike other countries considered here, Uganda has experienced an increase in the fraction of output generated by agriculture over the past several decades. In 1965, agriculture accounted for 52 percent of total output; by 1987, the share was 76 percent. As of 1980, 86 percent of the labor force was in agriculture. Major food crops include maize, millet, plantains, sorghum, pulses, and tubers. Coffee and cotton account for nearly all of Ugandan exports. Some tea is also exported.

As shown in Figure 5-17, Uganda saw erratic growth between 1960 and 1972, and then a severe decline between 1972 and 1980. There appears to have been some rebound in the early 1980s, but the decline resumed after 1983.[24] Political instability, civil war, and economic mismanagement, rather than exogenous economic factors, were the source of the economic decline of Uganda in the 1970s. In fact, the high rates of growth enjoyed by neighboring countries with similar production structures and exports imply that Uganda might have done well during the 1970s. Ugandan terms of trade were strong between 1974 and 1979 because coffee and cotton prices were high.

Yet, agricultural output fell during the 1970s (United Nations Development Program/World Bank, 1989). The decline was particularly severe for export crops, as farmers shifted from cash-crop production into subsistence farming. Coffee exports fell from 158,000 metric tons in 1965 to 110,000 metric tons in 1980, and cotton exports from 69,000 to 2,000 metric tons. Producer prices for these crops declined almost continuously through the 1970s. Real producer prices for coffee had lost three-quarters of their 1972 values by 1981, and producer prices for cotton plummeted even more.[25] Agricultural output was also adversely affected by a breakdown in transport and agricultural extension services. In general, gross domestic investment was exceptionally low during the 1970s; it was only 6 percent of GDP in 1980.

---

[24]As discussed in Appendix A, the data on per capita GDP for Uganda are especially suspect. In contrast to the other countries, for which we used data from the Penn World Table, for Uganda we relied on a newer data set from the World Bank. Although different data sources yield different numbers for Ugandan per capita output in the 1980s, the general pattern of a severe decline in the 1970s is common to all standard data sources.

[25]Unfortunately, continuous time series of producer prices of coffee and cotton are not available for Uganda, so we were not able to use these prices in our analysis.

Economic performance in the first half of the 1980s was mixed. In 1981, Uganda adopted an economic recovery program that included a devaluation, removal of many price controls, and increases in producer prices. Real producer prices for coffee and cotton were increased more than ninefold between 1981 and 1983. Export quantities increased in response. As discussed in footnote 24, different data sources recorded quite different measures of growth in incomes during this period. However, the supporting evidence indicates that the economy was in recovery in the early 1980s. In 1984, the economic recovery program began to falter, and in 1985 there was a coup followed by civil war. There is little reliable information on how living standards changed between 1981 and 1985 in Uganda, especially for the poorest segments of the population.

In what follows, we examine whether demographic outcomes are related to economic indicators. The economic indicators include per capita GDP, terms of trade and export quantum indices, and the world prices of coffee and cotton. But the international economic environment has played only a minor role in the determination of Ugandan living standards. Political instability and economic policy have been far more important, and the measures of world prices do not reflect these factors. Per capita GDP should, in theory, serve as a good measure of average living standards; but measurement error in per capita output is likely to be severe, potentially biasing our results. The export quantum also serves as a general measure of living standards and may affect both rural and urban areas; however, because the sample size was small in the case of mortality and information was lacking on residence at age 12 in the cases of marriage and fertility, we were not able to do the analysis separately for urban and rural samples in Uganda.

Demographic Outcomes

Uganda made little progress in reducing child mortality in the 1970s and 1980s (Hill, 1993), and the total fertility rate remained above seven children per woman in the late 1980s (Cohen, 1993). The age at marriage of women may have increased by a few months in the last few decades, according to some evidence (van de Walle, 1993).

Our results, as shown in Table 5-28, indicate a slight but significant trend upward in mortality over the 1970-1987 period. Figure 5-17 also demonstrates this trend from 1970 to the early 1980s, but suggests that survival may have improved in the mid-1980s. There is no significant year-to-year variation around the trend. The results of the analysis including economic variables are mixed. As shown in Table 5-29, EXQ had negative effects on mortality, whereas the real world price of cotton (WPCOT) had positive effects.

The log odds of marriage declined significantly from 1960 to 1987, but once again there was no significant variation around the trend and the economic variables had no effects (Table 5-30).

Similarly, the log odds of first birth showed a significant downward trend, but no significant year-to-year variation net of the trend.[26] However, two of the economic variables, real GDP per capita and the export quantum index, have significant positive effects on first births, as was hypothesized (Table 5-31).

For second births, there is also a slight, but significant trend downward in the log odds, but no variation net of the trend. Real GDP per capita has a positive effect on the probability of a second birth, as does the quantity of exports (Table 5-32).

These results indicate that variations in macroeconomic factors from year to year have had no influence on child mortality and marriage in Uganda. These results, however, are for economic variation *net* of trend, and although beyond the scope of this study, it may well be that the downward trends in standards of living are associated with the increases in child mortality that are apparent in Figure 5-17. However, the increasing importance of AIDS in Uganda confounds this interpretation. For first and second births, our results indicate that short-term economic variations net of trend, especially as reflected by GDP per capita and the quantity of exports, have been positively associated with these outcomes, as we hypothesized. Even so, given the difficulties in measuring GDP in Uganda, these results should be interpreted with care.

---

[26]In the model with education, there is a significant variation around the trend ($p = .09$).

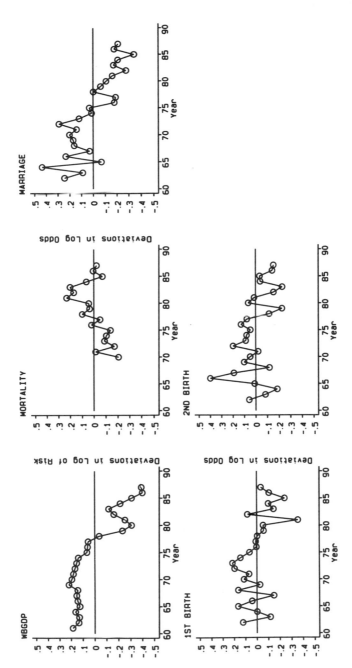

FIGURE 5-17 Time pattern of deviations in the logarithm of real gross domestic product per capita and the estimated demographic outcomes, total sample, Uganda.

TABLE 5-28   Effects of Time Period on Demographic Outcomes, Uganda

	Child Mortality[a]	First Marriage[b]	First Birth[b]	Second Birth[b]
Trend	.01	−.02	−.01	−.01
Tests (p-values)[c]				
No trend	.04**	.00**	.00**	.01**
No variation	.23	.00**	.01**	.43
No variation net of trend	.40	.37	.10	.75
Number				
Children	16,074	—	—	—
Women	—	4,730	4,730	3,493

[a]In mortality analysis, age of child is controlled. Period of analysis is 1970-1987.

[b]In marriage and first-birth analyses, age of woman is controlled; in second-birth analysis, age of woman and interval since first birth are controlled. Period of analysis is 1962-1987.

[c] * indicates a p-value of < .10; ** means a p-value of < .05.

TABLE 5-29   Effects of Economic Variables on Child Mortality, Uganda

	WBGDP Total	EXQ Total	TT Total	WPCOF Total	WPCOT Total
Coefficients by lag					
0	−0.23	−0.09	−0.01	0.06	0.25*
1	0.26	−0.06	−0.04	−0.06	−0.00
2	−0.90	−0.33**	0.11	0.12	0.16
Sum of coefficients	−0.88	−0.49	0.06	0.12	0.41
Tests (p-values)[a]					
Coefficients are zero	.12	.02**	.90	.63	.26
Sum of coefficients is zero	.12	.00**	.75	.26	.07*

NOTES: Age of child and year are controlled. WBGDP, real gross domestic product per capita, 1970-1987; EXQ, export quantum index, 1970-1987; TT, terms of trade index, 1970-1987; WPCOF, real world price of coffee, 1970-1987; WPCOT, real world price of cotton, 1970-1987.

[a] * indicates a p-value of < .10; ** means a p-value of < .05.

TABLE 5-30   Effects of Economic Variables on Marriage, Uganda

	WBGDP Total	EXQ Total	TT Total	WPCOF Total	WPCOT Total
Coefficients by lag					
0	−0.06	0.06	−0.09	−0.13	−0.05
1	0.08	0.11	0.12	0.09	−0.10
2	0.14	−0.03	0.12	0.03	−0.03
Sum of coefficients	0.16	0.15	0.14	−0.01	−0.17
Tests (p-values)^a Coefficients are zero	.85	.51	.28	.35	.58
Sum of coefficients is zero	.56	.17	.35	.94	.28

NOTES: Age of woman and year are controlled. WBGDP, real gross domestic product per capita, 1962-1987; EXQ, export quantum index, 1962-1987; TT, terms of trade index, 1962-1987; WPCOF, real world price of coffee, 1962-1987; WPCOT, real world price of cotton, 1962-1987.

^{a} * indicates a p-value of < .10; ** means a p-value of < .05.

TABLE 5-31   Effects of Economic Variables on First Births, Uganda

	WBGDP Total	EXQ Total	TT Total	WPCOF Total	WPCOT Total
Coefficients by lag					
0	0.41	0.26**	−0.03	0.02	0.14
1	0.11	0.05	−0.08	−0.05	−0.13
2	0.09	−0.01	0.06	0.00	0.04
Sum of coefficients	0.61	0.31	−0.05	−0.02	0.05
Tests (p-values)^a Coefficients are zero	.08*	.03**	.85	.97	.62
Sum of coefficients is zero	.03**	.00**	.75	.78	.77

NOTES: Age of woman and year are controlled. WBGDP, real gross domestic product per capita, 1962-1987; EXQ, export quantum index, 1962-1987; TT, terms of trade index, 1962-1987; WPCOF, real world price of coffee, 1962-1987; WPCOT, real world price of cotton, 1962-1987.

^{a} * indicates a p-value of < .10; ** means a p-value of < .05.

TABLE 5-32   Effects of Economic Variables on Second Births, Uganda

	WBGDP Total	EXQ Total	TT Total	WPCOF Total	WPCOT Total
Coefficients by lag					
0	1.02*	−0.17	0.07	0.03	0.06
1	−1.53**	0.03	−0.01	0.02	0.15
2	1.25**	0.32*	−0.20	−0.05	−0.16
Sum of coefficients	0.75	0.18	−0.14	0.01	0.06
Tests (*p*-values)[a]					
Coefficients are zero	.11	.06*	.52	.96	.63
Sum of coefficients is zero	.04**	.23	.52	.97	.79

NOTES: Age of woman, interval since first birth, and year are controlled. WBGDP, real gross domestic product per capita, 1962-1987; EXQ, export quantum index, 1962-1987; TT, terms of trade index, 1962-1987; WPCOF, real world price of coffee, 1962-1987; WPCOT, real world price of cotton, 1962-1987.

[a] * indicates a *p*-value of < .10; ** means a *p*-value of < .05.

6

Cross-National Comparisons

It is reasonable to expect that the processes that link an economic change to a demographic outcome operate in similar ways in different countries, with some variation introduced by differences in economic structures and policies between countries. It is therefore of interest to compare the responses of demographic parameters to given economic indicators across countries and attempt to identify common patterns. The comparison also serves to reinforce conclusions that may not be statistically significant country by country because sample sizes are limited, but whose consistency across countries suggests a real effect. By the same token, the comparison may undermine a country-specific conclusion that is contradicted in another country. The comparison can thus be seen as an informal meta-analysis, lacking a formal procedure for significance testing but contributing to confidence in the overall results.

To make these comparisons we have selected six standardized economic indicators that capture different dimensions of economic reversal. The first indicator, real gross domestic product (GDP) per capita, provides a general indicator of economic performance and is available for all seven countries. The second is an index of the quantity of exports, which reflects the performance of the economy's external sector, excluding price effects. The third is terms of trade, which introduces the price dimension in the external sector and can plausibly be regarded as exogenous. Both the export quantum and the terms of trade are available for all countries studied except Botswana. The fourth indicator is the world price of a country's main agricultural export, which is a component of terms of trade and, once again, exogenously determined. Again, only Botswana lacks this indicator. For Ghana, Nigeria, and Togo, the product is cocoa; for Kenya and Uganda, it is coffee; and for Senegal, groundnuts. The fifth indicator is the world price of a country's main mineral export, again a component of terms of trade and exogenously determined. Three of our countries, Ghana, Kenya, and Uganda, do not export important quantities of any mineral and so do not contribute to this comparison. The Botswana economy is driven almost entirely by the export of a single mineral, diamonds, for which no series on world prices is available; however, Botswana depends so heavily on diamonds that those prices probably covary almost perfectly with GDP. Thus this indicator is used for only three countries: Nigeria (oil), Senegal (phosphates), and Togo (phosphates). The sixth indicator is the producer price of a country's main agricultural export crop; a major plank of structural adjustment programs is to improve price incentives in the productive sectors of the economy, so this variable may capture adjustment effects per se. This indicator is available for all countries except Botswana and Uganda.

Besides presenting results for the total samples for each of the economic indicators, we summarize results for the urban and rural samples, to explore whether the effects of certain indicators are more pronounced in one type of locale than in the other. Because the sample sizes in urban areas were small or information on residence was insufficient, we could not make this urban-rural contrast for Botswana and Uganda for any of the demographic outcomes or for Kenya for child mortality.

The basic method of presentation used in this chapter is a scatter plot of the response coefficients of a demographic indicator to each economic indicator with lags of zero, one, and two years, plus the sum of the elasticities over all three lags (the coefficients can be viewed as elasticities; see Chapter 4). Thus the plotted points for lags of zero, one, and two years indicate the magnitude and timing of any response, whereas the points for the sum indicate whether the effects identified are merely timing effects or they influence longer-term levels. Elasticities that are significantly different from zero are shown by crosses, whereas nonsignificant values are marked by circles.

INFANT AND CHILD MORTALITY

Panel A of Figure 6-1 shows the estimates of linear trends for child mortality for the total sample, urban children, and rural children. respectively. For the total sample, all the trend estimates are significantly different from zero; they range from a 1 percent annual increase (for Uganda) to a 5 percent annual decline (for Botswana). The median decline is 3 percent per year. The percentage declines in urban areas range from 0 to 3 percent[1]

---

[1]The trend estimates for urban Senegal and Togo are both zero (and insignificantly different from zero) and thus are graphed one on top of the other.

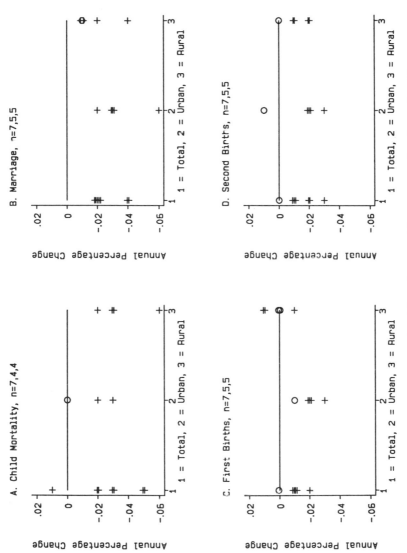

FIGURE 6-1 Estimated time trends of four demographic outcomes, by place of residence.

and appear to have been outpaced by declines in rural areas, which range from 2 to 5 percent. Excluding the special case of Uganda, child mortality appears to have declined throughout the 1970s and 1980s. However, because the trend measure is a linear one, the analysis would not pick up any trend reversal in the latter part of the time period covered.

Figures 6-2 to 6-7 summarize relationships between child mortality risks and the six standard economic indicators across the seven countries studied. If they are available, results are given separately for urban, rural, and total populations. In the case of child mortality, a negative coefficient indicates that mortality falls as the economic indicator improves, and thus that mortality rises as the economic indicator declines.

For the total sample, real GDP per capita appears to have a "down-up-down" relationship at lags of zero, one, and two years, with a generally negative net sum. Thus child mortality appears to be higher than trend in the year of a relatively low GDP value and two years later, but lower than trend one year later. The sums of the coefficients indicate that overall mortality is higher than trend over the years following a low value of GDP per capita. For the total sample, the median elasticity is –0.2 at lag zero, +0.3 at lag one, and –0.3 at lag two, with a median net sum of –0.3. However, the elasticities are significantly different from zero only at the two-year lag for three of the seven countries and for the net sum for only one country. The urban and rural samples seem to show the same down-up-down pattern, with a negative net sum in urban areas, but no clear net sum for rural areas. The estimates generally are not significantly different from zero.

The results for export quantum (Figure 6-3) show a somewhat similar pattern, the clearest effects being a positive elasticity at lag one counterbalanced by a negative elasticity at lag two. The overall magnitudes of the elasticities are smaller than they are for GDP per capita, and the net sums are no longer clearly negative. However, the export quantum produces a larger number of significant elasticities than does any other economic indicator, even though some of them have contradictory signs.

Despite having a number of elasticities that are significant at the country level, the terms of trade and child mortality (Figure 6-4) have no clear relationship across the countries, either at any individual lag or across all lags. A similar conclusion appears to hold for the world prices of the major agricultural export (Figure 6-5). For the total sample, the elasticities for all lags are spread around zero, although there are a few significant results for individual countries. The urban and rural estimated elasticities show more spread around zero, but no clear pattern. The results for the world prices of the major mineral export (Figure 6-6) similarly fail to show any clear pattern, though the total country results hint at a down-up-down pattern, and a net sum close to zero. The graphs for the producer price of the major

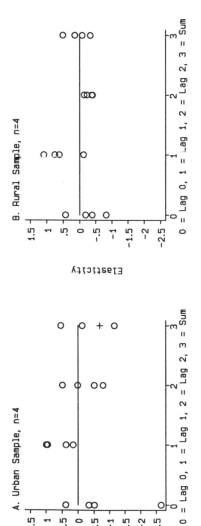

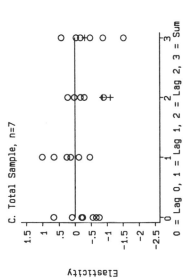

FIGURE 6-2 Estimated coefficients and sums of coefficients for models of child mortality including real gross domestic product, by place of residence.

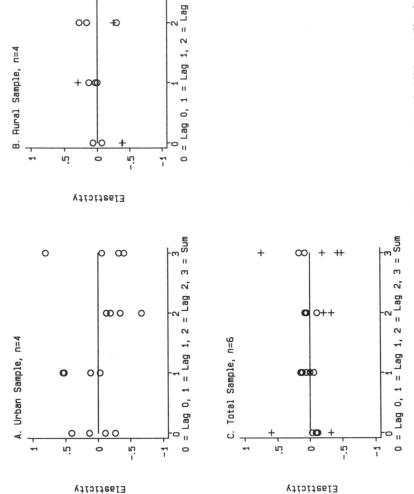

FIGURE 6-3 Estimated coefficients and sums of coefficients for models of child mortality including the export quantum index, by place of residence.

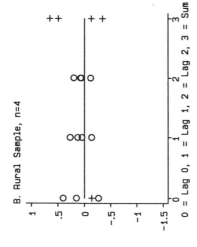

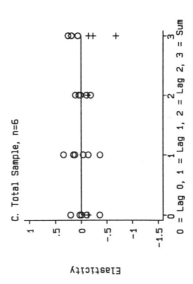

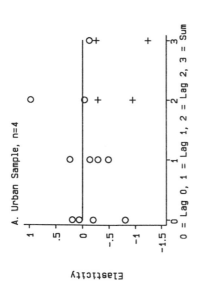

FIGURE 6-4 Estimated coefficients and sums of coefficients for models of child mortality including the terms of trade index, by place of residence.

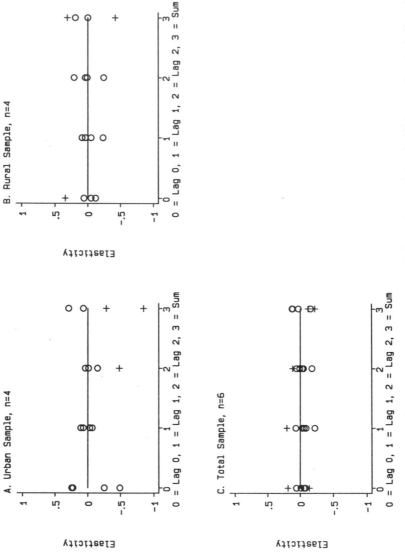

FIGURE 6-5 Estimated coefficients and sums of coefficients for models of child mortality including the world price of a major agricultural export, by place of residence.

143

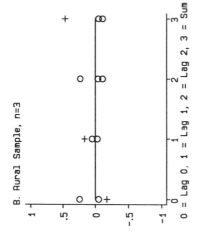

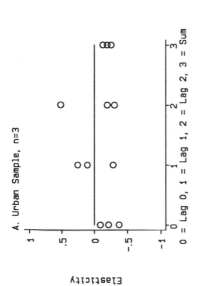

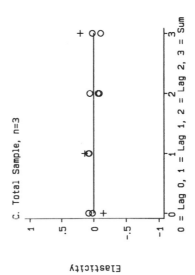

FIGURE 6-6 Estimated coefficients and sums of coefficients for models of child mortality including the world price of a major mineral export, by place of residence.

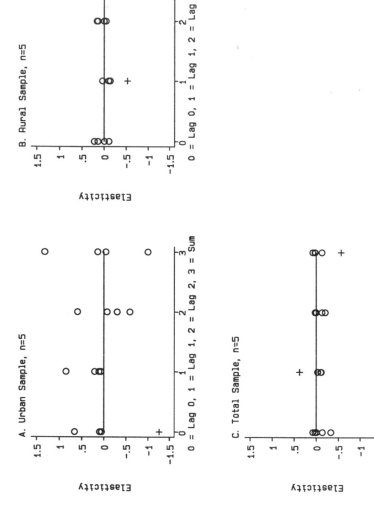

FIGURE 6-7   Estimated coefficients and sums of coefficients for models of child mortality including the producer price of a major agricultural export, by place of residence.

agricultural export (Figure 6-7) again suggest a down-up-down pattern with no clear net sum for the total sample and for urban areas, but a "flat-down-up" pattern for rural areas, with no net sum. Thus falling (or rising) producer prices appear to be associated with rising (or falling) child mortality risks in the next year in rural areas and more or less immediately in urban areas.

In summary, child mortality in sub-Saharan Africa does seem to be affected to some extent by economic conditions in the short run. The effect is largest and clearest when using real GDP per capita as the economic indicator, though it appears in dampened form for other indicators also. The pattern is for child mortality to be above trend in a year in which GDP per capita falls, to be below trend in the following year (lag one), and to be higher again in the year after that (lag two). The effects of the indicators differ little between rural and urban areas, with the single exception of the producer price variables, which appear to have major negative effects on child mortality at lag one in rural areas, but at lags zero and two in urban areas.

MARRIAGE

Panel B of Figure 6-1 summarizes the effects of the time trend on the log odds of first marriage. For all countries, the trend in first marriage odds is downward in the total, urban, and rural samples. This trend is significantly different from zero for all but one country-residence combination (Ghana rural) at the 1 percent level. Thus, our analysis of Demographic and Health Survey data indicates that age at marriage has been rising since 1960 in all seven countries studied,[2] and that the pace of change has been faster in urban than in rural areas.

Figures 6-8 to 6-13 show elasticities of the log odds of first marriage to the six economic indicators with lags of zero, one, and two years, and for the sum across the three lags, for the total sample, and for urban and rural samples separately. The patterns for real per capita GDP (Figure 6-8) are not very clear: There appear to be positive elasticities at lag one (and possibly at lag zero), nothing much at lag two, and a generally positive sum, particularly when significantly different from zero. Neither export quantum (Figure 6-9) nor terms of trade (Figure 6-10) show much pattern for individual lags, but the sums tend to be positive, once again, especially when significant.

---

[2]This result is quite different from that of van de Walle (1993), who finds only limited evidence of increasing age of marriage, given the difficulties of making comparisons over time and across data sets. It should be noted that our result may differ in part because of the assumption in our models of unvarying effects of age over time on the log odds of marriage.

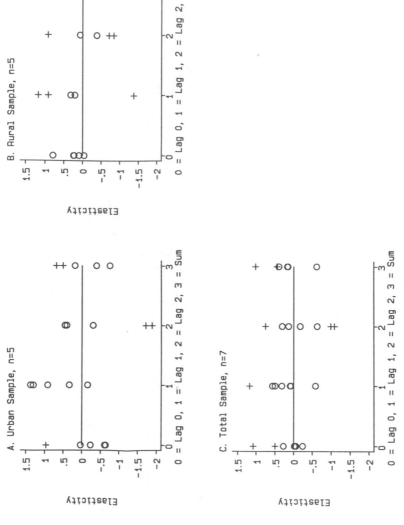

FIGURE 6-8 Estimated coefficients and sums of coefficients for models of marriage including real gross domestic product, by place of residence.

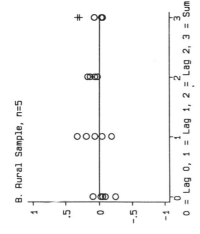

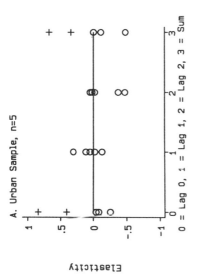

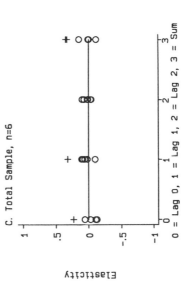

FIGURE 6-9 Estimated coefficients and sums of coefficients for models of marriage including the export quantum index, by place of residence.

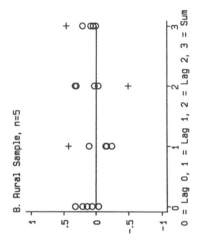

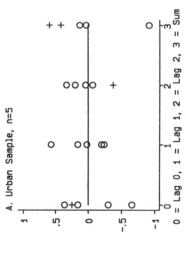

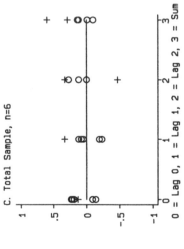

FIGURE 6-10 Estimated coefficients and sums of coefficients for models of marriage including the terms of trade index, by place of residence.

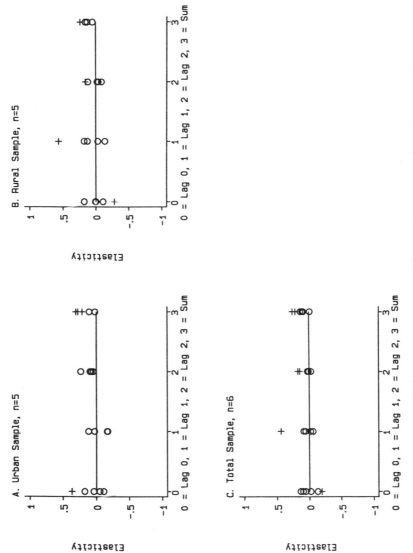

FIGURE 6-11 Estimated coefficients and sums of coefficients for models of marriage including the world price of a major agricultural export, by place of residence.

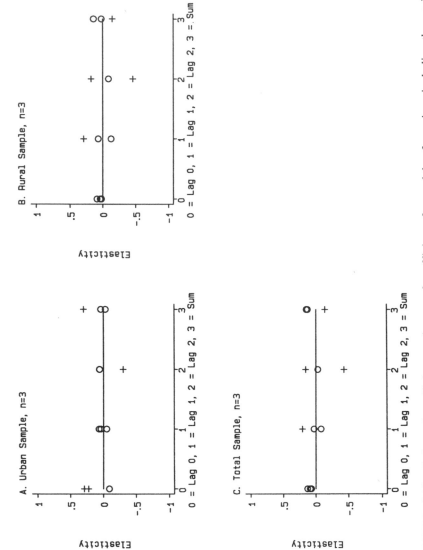

FIGURE 6-12 Estimated coefficients and sums of coefficients for models of marriage including the world price of a major mineral export, by place of residence.

151

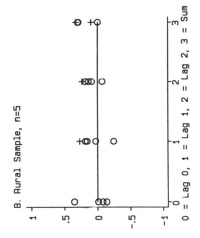

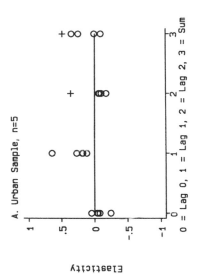

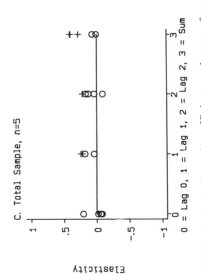

FIGURE 6-13 Estimated coefficients and sums of coefficients for models of marriage including the producer price of a major agricultural export, by place of residence.

No very clear lag-specific effects of the world price of a country's major agricultural export appear (Figure 6-11), though the sums across all lags are positive for total, urban, and rural samples, often significantly so. The effects of mineral prices (Figure 6-12) are less clear-cut still: Even the sums vary around zero. The producer price of the main agricultural export crop (Figure 6-13) appears to have little effect at lag zero and lag two, but a positive effect at lag one that is at least as marked in urban as in rural areas. All the sums are positive except for urban Nigeria, often significantly so.

To summarize, the effects of economic conditions on the log odds of first marriage are not entirely clear-cut in our analysis, although in general improved economic conditions are associated with higher odds of first marriage over a three-year period. Marriage odds appear to respond quite rapidly to economic conditions, typically in the same or the following year. The economic indicators with the clearest effects are real per capita GDP and the producer prices of the major agricultural export; thus marriages seem to respond relatively more to domestic than to international conditions, which are captured more purely in the export quantum, terms of trade, and world prices.

FIRST BIRTH

Figure 6-1, Panel C, summarizes the time trends in the log odds of first birth. Overall, those odds have been declining (and age at first birth rising) in all countries except Botswana and Nigeria. The effects appear, however, to be concentrated almost entirely in urban areas with negative trends for all five countries for which the urban analysis was possible. Little change is evident in rural areas (two significantly positive values versus one significantly negative value). Thus, some secular trend toward later entry into childbearing is apparent in urban areas, although it is less marked than the delay in entry into first union.

Relationships to economic variables are summarized in Figures 6-14 to 6-19. The relationships with real per capita GDP (Figure 6-14) at individual lags appear to have no clear pattern, although all the significant elasticities for lags zero and one are positive, and the significant elasticities at lag two are negative. Sums across all years are always positive for the total and rural samples and are generally positive for the urban sample (the only exception is urban Senegal, and its estimate is not significantly different from zero). Thus, good economic times seem to encourage people to begin childbearing, with some compensating effect two years later.

The export quantum (Figure 6-15) is associated, particularly in rural areas, with some positive response at lag zero and a negative response at lag one. Sums tend to be positive, especially where significant. A response to the export quantum at lag zero, given the lag inherent in childbearing,

153

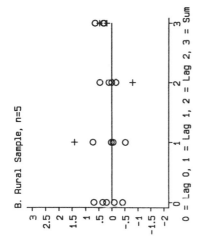

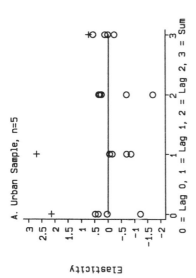

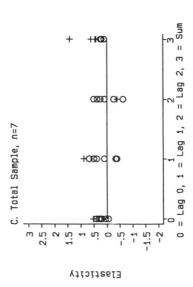

FIGURE 6-14 Estimated coefficients and sums of coefficients for models of first births including real gross domestic product, by place of residence.

154

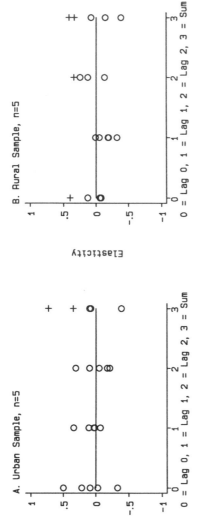

FIGURE 6-15 Estimated coefficients and sums of coefficients for models of first births including the export quantum index, by place of residence.

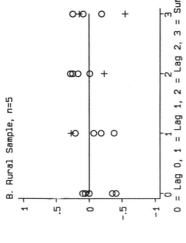

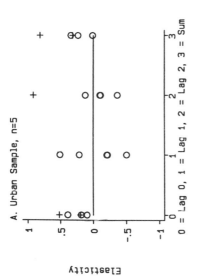

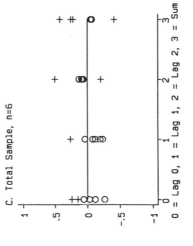

FIGURE 6-16 Estimated coefficients and sums of coefficients for models of first births including the terms of trade index, by place of residence.

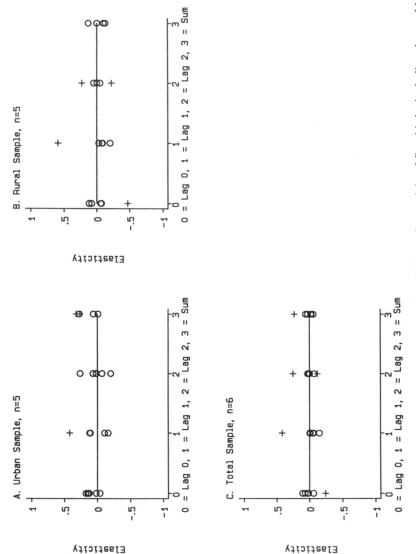

FIGURE 6-17 Estimated coefficients and sums of coefficients for models of first births including the world price of a major agricultural export, by place of residence.

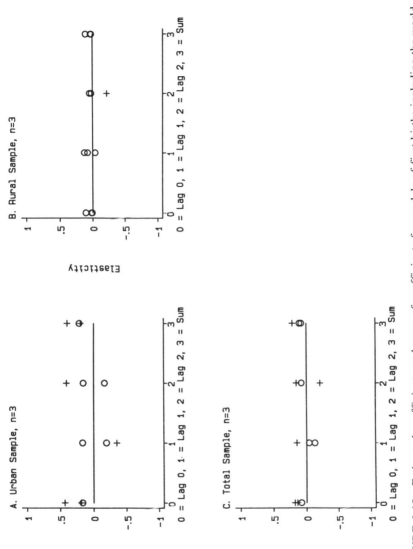

FIGURE 6-18 Estimated coefficients and sums of coefficients for models of first births including the world price of a major mineral export, by place of residence.

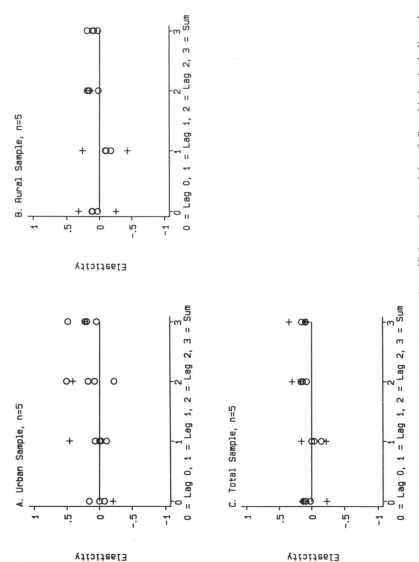

FIGURE 6-19 Estimated coefficients and sums of coefficients for models of first births including the producer price of a major agricultural export, by place of residence.

seems a trifle unlikely unless potential parents are good forecasters. Terms of trade (Figure 6-16) show no pattern either at individual years or for the sum, in rural areas or for the total sample; but they show a positive effect at lag zero and for the sum in urban areas. Changes in the terms of trade may affect urban households before they affect the rest of the country, perhaps through effects on government revenues and expenditures.

The world price of a country's major agricultural export (Figure 6-17) appears to have very little effect on the log odds of first birth. There is perhaps the suggestion of a significant positive effect on the net sum in urban areas (though, surprisingly, not in rural areas), but no clear lag-specific effects are evident. The effects of the world price of a country's major mineral export (Figure 6-18) have the same pattern, but much more strongly. The effect is strongest in urban areas, where both the sums and the responses at lag zero are clearly positive. Rural areas show little effect, and the total sample reflects the urban results, only in weaker form. Real producer prices (Figure 6-19) show a very different pattern: No urban response is evident, but positive responses appear at lag two and in sum for both rural and total samples.

In summary, first births appear to respond positively to economic fluctuations. The effects of changes in world prices of mineral exports are particularly clear at short lags in urban areas, and, to a lesser extent, the same is true of movements in world prices for major agricultural export crops. Fairly clear effects also appear at long lags in rural areas for changes in producer prices of major agricultural products.

SECOND BIRTH

Panel D of Figure 6-1 summarizes the time trends in the log odds of second birth. Almost all the trend coefficients (and all the significant ones) are negative, indicating that the odds of second birth have declined since the early 1960s. The trend is particularly marked in urban areas, but, unlike the case of first births, it is also quite clear in rural areas.

Figures 6-20 to 6-25 summarize the relationships between economic indicators and the log odds of second birth by area of residence. For neither per capita real GDP (Figure 6-20) nor export quantum (Figure 6-21) is there any clear pattern of effects on second births for individual lags, but per capita real GDP does seem to be positively associated with the sum for the total sample. Terms of trade (Figure 6-22) appear to exert a positive effect at lags zero and two for the total and urban samples, with positive sums in both cases. The effects of world prices of major agricultural exports (Figure 6-23) and major mineral exports (Figure 6-24) show no clear timing pattern, but these variables appear to be associated again with positive sums. The effects of producer prices of major agricultural exports (Figure 6-25)

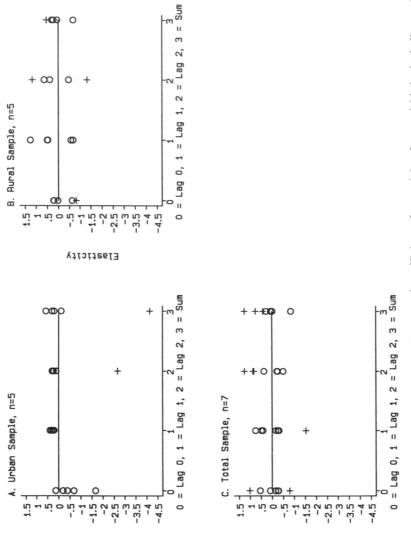

FIGURE 6-20 Estimated coefficients and sums of coefficients for models of second births including real gross domestic product, by place of residence.

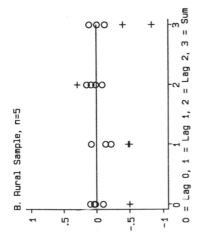

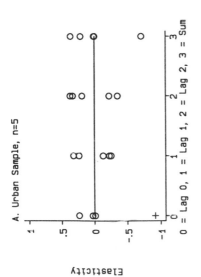

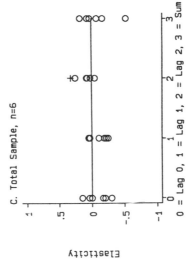

FIGURE 6-21 Estimated coefficients and sums of coefficients for models of second births including the export quantum index, by place of residence.

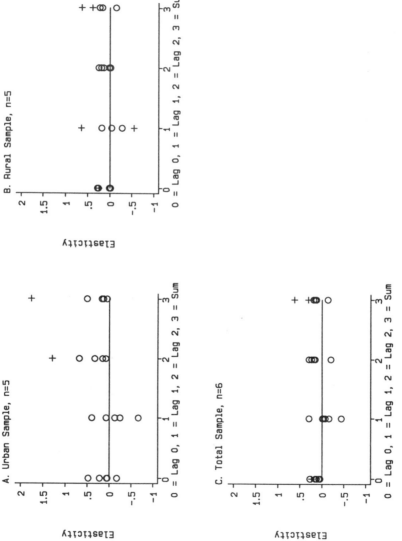

FIGURE 6-22 Estimated coefficients and sums of coefficients for models of second births including the terms of trade index, by place of residence.

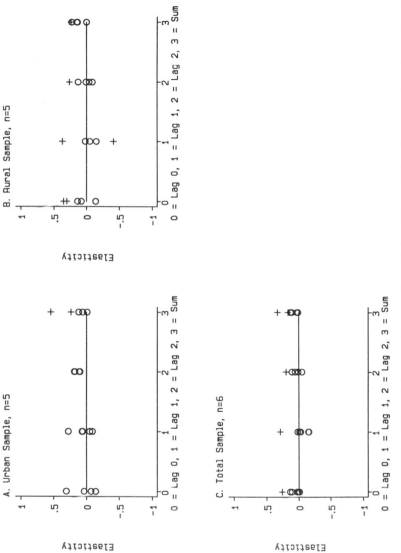

FIGURE 6-23 Estimated coefficients and sums of coefficients for models of second births including the world price of a major agricultural export, by place of residence.

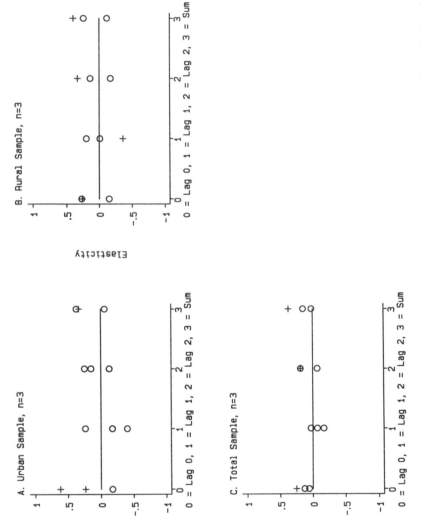

FIGURE 6-24 Estimated coefficients and sums of coefficients for models of second births including the world price of a major mineral export, by place of residence.

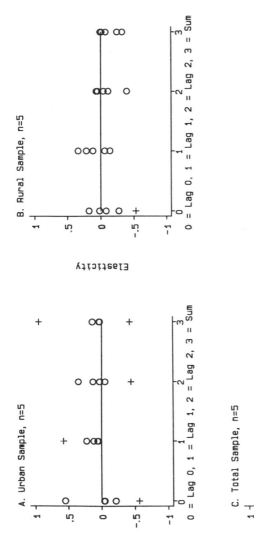

FIGURE 6-25 Estimated coefficients and sums of coefficients for models of second births including the producer price of a major agricultural export, by place of residence.

once again trace a down-up-down pattern that is particularly evident for the total sample. Thus, the odds of second birth appear to respond positively to producer prices with a one-year lag. However, the signs of the sums are mixed.

In summary, the log odds of having a second birth appear on average to be positively associated with economic indicators, although no clear timing pattern of the effects emerges except for producer prices, the response to which seems to lag about one year.

CONCLUSION

The analysis shows that all the demographic outcomes studied—child mortality, first marriage, first birth, and second birth—have been declining in almost all the countries studied. In addition, at least some systematic variations around these trends have been associated with short-term fluctuations in economic conditions. Overall, child mortality tends to increase as economic conditions deteriorate; the response is most evident for the general indicator of economic condition, real per capita GDP. The three family-formation variables—marriage, first birth, and second birth--appear to vary positively with economic conditions, often in the same year, and they appear to respond most strongly in urban areas to price variables. These conclusions, however, are somewhat speculative. The estimated effects are by no means uniform or uniformly significant across countries, partly because of genuine differences across countries and partly because of small sample sizes. However, there seems little doubt that economic conditions affect the demographic outcomes considered in the analysis, although the analysis is certainly not precise enough to distinguish between the effects of general economic malaise and the effects of, for example, adjustment policies.

7

Caveats and Conclusions

This study has attempted to ascertain the existence and extent of demographic effects of economic reversals in recent decades in seven sub-Saharan African countries. We selected the countries to be studied—Botswana, Ghana, Kenya, Nigeria, Senegal, Togo, and Uganda—not because they represent sub-Saharan Africa as a whole but because they represent a variety of economic and demographic experiences. Although they are all low- or lower-middle-income countries, some have been more severely affected than others by economic downturns in the 1970s and 1980s. Moreover, their economies have quite different structures, exhibiting different degrees of diversification and government intervention. In all except Uganda child survival has improved, but in only two—Botswana and Kenya—has total fertility declined significantly.

Ideally we would have analyzed long time series of vital events in each of these countries and linked variations in the numbers of those events to changes in economic conditions. Instead, we have had to rely on retrospective reports of individual women about their marriages and the births and deaths of their children.

In some cases the economic data have also not been ideal. Data on gross domestic product may not provide a good measure of year-to-year economic variation in economies with large informal or subsistence sectors. Several of the economic indicators that we have used—the export quantum index, the terms of trade, and world commodity prices—measure changes over time in the international economic environment for each country. We would have preferred better indicators of variations of economic conditions within countries. For example, except for data on rainfall in Senegal, we have been unable to include indicators of environmental conditions that are likely to be important in primarily agricultural economies.

Nor have we been able to delineate the distributional aspects of economic change as it has affected different segments of each population, the rich versus the poor, for example. We have used producer prices as proxies for standards of living in rural areas, but the particular commodities are of varying importance to each economy and the proportion of the labor force employed in each may not be large. Still, we recognized that nonproducers of a commodity might experience spillover effects from changes in its price.

Also missing from our analysis are measures of the way government responses to economic reversals have affected the well-being of the populations. But time series of public expenditures on social, health, and family planning services were not long enough for our purposes.

Furthermore, the available data, both demographic and economic, may not permit a timing of events precise enough to analyze true short-term variation. For example, retrospective demographic data of the sort that we have used involve potential error in dating of events, which may shift events from one calendar year to another. Also, some of the economic indicators that we have used may change only slowly over time, and spillover effects from one segment of the economy to another may also occur with different lags. Accordingly, our methods may not be able to detect year-to-year changes in economic conditions; they are likely, however, to be sensitive to more persistent economic shocks.

Moreover, the data available to us have dictated the methodology we have used and the assumptions inherent therein. Once again, the paths we have taken are not necessarily ones we preferred, but we believe that they represent reasonable compromises with reality.

These caveats certainly suggest directions for further data collection and research. However, we believe that the results of our analysis indeed indicate that the economic reversals experienced in sub-Saharan Africa have affected child mortality, first marriage, and first and second births, albeit with considerable variation in the size and pattern of the effects. To simplify the discussion and to avoid overinterpretation of individual coefficients, our concluding observations are based on the results for the sums of the coefficients of the current and lagged values of the economic variables.

The effects of poor economic conditions on child mortality are clearest for Ghana (especially in rural areas) and Nigeria (especially in urban areas). The results are mixed for Kenya, Senegal, Togo, and Uganda: Some economic indicators have negative effects, whereas others have positive ones. Variations in economic conditions appear to have had no effects on variations in child mortality net of trend in Botswana.

The positive association between economic conditions and the odds of marrying for the first time are also quite clear in Botswana, Senegal, and Togo (especially in urban areas). Economic factors generally have positive effects on marriage also in Kenya and Nigeria, but there are exceptions. The patterns of marriage in Ghana and Uganda do not seem to be associated with any of the economic indicators.

Of the four demographic outcomes, first births show the strongest links to economic conditions. In all our countries except Kenya variations in one or more of the economic indicators that were available display a positive relation to variation net of trend in the odds of first birth, and none shows negative relations. The results are mixed in Kenya. Overall, where the comparison is possible, effects are more significant in urban than rural areas.

On the other hand, the results for second births are perhaps the weakest. For Botswana, Ghana, and Uganda, the significant relations with the economic indicators are all positive, but the results are mixed for Nigeria and Senegal. For Togo, none of the economic variables affected the odds of second births, and only one did in Kenya.

Nigeria stands out as the country with the strongest across-the-board effects of economic reversals. We believe that the dominance of one commodity, oil, in the economy and the severity of the economic shock in Nigeria account for this finding. Botswana's economy is also quite dependent on a single commodity, diamonds, whose prices briefly declined in the 1980s; but among our countries, Botswana stands out as an economic and demographic success no doubt in part because of its government's careful management of revenues. Kenya, which did experience a recession in the 1980s, exhibited relatively few demographic effects of economic changes, most likely because its economic base is quite diversified.

Evaluating the effects of economic reversals on subnational groups, such as urban and rural residents, has been difficult. In some cases, the data available to us did not allow such a division of the samples. For Ghana, the effects on child mortality, first births, and second births have been most apparent in rural areas. For Kenya, where the effects are generally small, the results are slightly stronger in rural than in urban areas. The results in Nigeria are slightly stronger in urban than in rural areas, but the effects of economic reversal appear to be pervasive. For Senegal and Togo, the effects on marriage and first births have been felt primarily in urban areas, especially those of world prices. These results are consistent with our hypothesis that in countries such as Senegal and Togo whose governments control producer prices, urban areas will exhibit greater demographic effects than will rural areas. The reasoning is that in these countries government revenues and expenditures respond to changes in world prices and that urban areas are the primary beneficiaries of government expenditures. Where urban effects are relatively strong, it could also be that rural households are better able to adapt to international price variations by transferring resources across time and space or by shifting away from activities that have become less profitable.

In conclusion, changes in economic conditions in recent decades in the seven sub-Saharan African countries we studied have been reflected in variations net of trend in child mortality, first marriages, and first and second births. We have not attempted to link the deterioration of economic conditions to the implementation of structural adjustment programs, some of which may have had positive effects, or to analyze the causes of long-term demographic trends. Rather, our goal has been to reach a better understanding of the associations between short-term variations in economic and demographic indicators in Africa. Our analysis indicates that the lives of many people in sub-Saharan Africa were likely affected by economic reversals as they suffered the deaths of their children or made decisions to delay or forgo marriage and parenthood.

APPENDIXES

A

Economic Data

Tables A-1 through A-7 present selected data for each country. Table A-8 contains data on world commodity prices.

Data on Gross Domestic Product, Terms of Trade, and Export Quantities

GDP

Definition: real gross domestic product per capita.
Unit of measure: 1985 U.S. dollars.
Source: GDP is drawn from the Penn World Table (Mark 5).

The data source is described in more detail in "The Penn World Table (Mark 5): An Expanded Set of International Comparisons, 1950-1988" (Summers and Heston, 1991). The data source provides several measures of per capita GDP. For all countries, the measure based on a Laspeyres price index was used. This is the measure recommended for both cross-country and time-series comparisons of per capita GDP. The Laspeyres-based measure of GDP for Uganda yields growth rates of per capita GDP between 1980 and 1985 that are unrealistically high (for example, 1985 real GDP per capita is reported to be 2.79 times that in 1980). No other data source yields growth rates of this magnitude. Other measures of Ugandan per capita GDP provided in the Penn World Table (such as that based on a chain index) are also at odds with those from other data sources. To cross-check whether our results are sensitive to changes in measures of GDP, we experimented with yet another measure of real per capita gross domestic product, WBGDP (base year = 1980). It is drawn from the United Nations Development Program/World Bank (1989) and according to experts on Uganda provides a more realistic pattern over time. It appears in the last column of Table A-7 and is the measure we use in our statistical analysis.

TT

    Definition: terms of trade index.
    Unit of measure: index number, base year is 1980.
    Source: United Nations Committee on Trade and Development
      (various years).

The data are constructed from two time series. The earlier time series runs from 1960 to 1980, with a base year of 1975. A later time series runs from 1972 to 1988, with a base year of 1980. Terms of trade numbers from 1972 and on were taken directly from the later series. Terms of trade measures from 1960 to 1971 were taken from the earlier series. The earlier series was rebased by computing the average ratio between the two series in 1972 and 1973, and scaling the 1960-1971 numbers by this ratio.

EXQ

    Definition: export quantum index.
    Unit of measure: index number, base year is 1980.
    Source: United Nations Committee on Trade and Development
      (various years).

The export quantum indices were constructed in the same way as the terms of trade indices, described above.

Producer Prices and Other Data

All countries except Botswana and Uganda have at least one producer price series. For all countries, nominal producer prices (in local currency units) were converted to real U.S. dollars, with a base year of 1985. First, the data were converted to real (1985) prices in local currency units, using a consumer price deflator from the Penn World Table. Second, the data were converted to U.S. dollars using the purchasing power parity converter for consumption from the Penn World Table. Many of the producer price series are drawn from Banque Centrale des Etats de l'Afrique de l'Ouest (BCEAO) (various issues). Several series are from Hesp (1985), as noted below.

The sources for the producer price series (in local currency units) and other country-specific data series are as follows:

Ghana   PPCOC is the real producer price of cocoa. QCOC is tons of cocoa produced. The source for nominal prices and quantities produced is Azam and Besley (1989).

Kenya   PPCOF is the real producer price of coffee. The source for nominal prices is Kenya Central Bureau of Statistics (various years).

Nigeria   PPCOC is the real producer price of cocoa. The data on nominal prices from 1961 to 1968 are drawn from Hesp (1985). Later data are from Central Bank of Nigeria (various years).

Senegal   PPGN is the real producer price of groundnuts. The nominal price data are drawn from BCEAO (various issues). RAIN is millimeters of rainfall during the growing season in Diourbel, and is from Gersovitz (1986).

Togo   PPCOC and PPCOF are real producer prices for cocoa and coffee. The source for both series of nominal prices is Hesp (1985) for 1961-1972, and BCEAO (various issues) for later years.

WORLD COMMODITY PRICE DATA

The data on all commodity prices except groundnuts in Table A-8 are from World Bank (1986a) for the years 1960-1984; they were updated using unpublished data from the World Bank. All price series were deflated using the manufacturers unit value (MUV) index, from the same data source. This publication provides several price series for each commodity. We used these series: (1) cocoa—New York and London; (2) coffee—Angolan; (3) tea—average price for all tea; (4) cotton—"A" Index; (5) phosphate (phosphate rock)—Moroccan; (5) crude petroleum—Saudi Arabian.

Although World Bank (1986a) provides a price series for processed groundnut products (including groundnut oil and meal, as cited in Table 2-4 of Chapter 2), it does not publish a series for unprocessed groundnuts. We obtained a nominal price series for unprocessed groundnuts from the International Monetary Fund (1987) and used this for the statistical analysis. It was deflated by the MUV index and is presented in Table A-8.

Note that the units of measure for the world prices are not necessarily the same as those for producer prices.

TABLE A-1   Real Gross Domestic Product per Capita, Botswana, 1960-1986 (1985 U.S. dollars)

Year	GDP	Year	GDP
1960	510	1974	1,495
1961	534	1975	1,441
1962	559	1976	1,498
1963	572	1977	1,491
1964	593	1978	1,646
1965	550	1979	1,802
1966	573	1980	2,007
1967	693	1981	2,028
1968	774	1982	2,060
1969	786	1983	2,036
1970	964	1984	2,139
1971	976	1985	2,555
1972	1,089	1986	2,282
1973	1,300		

NOTE: See text for definition of variable and source of data.

TABLE A-2   Selected Economic Indicators, Ghana, 1960-1988

Year	GDP (1985 U.S. dollars)	TT (index, 1980 = 100)	EXQ (index, 1980 = 100)	PPCOC (1985 U.S. dollars per ton)	QCOC (tons)
1960	1,072	84	129	—	—
1961	1,105	73	149	1,882.8	409
1962	1,104	68	160	1,656.1	413
1963	1,113	68	147	1,464.3	428
1964	1,085	69	152	1,231.7	538
1965	1,088	58	179	993.0	401
1966	1,056	57	150	1,076.8	372
1967	1,074	68	141	1,305.8	423
1968	1,083	71	150	1,348.7	333
1969	1,121	84	123	1,276.4	419
1970	1,172	92	166	1,239.0	434
1971	1,193	69	158	1,134.0	477
1972	1,159	61	204	1,255.2	427
1973	1,119	66	221	1,313.2	357
1974	1,177	73	163	1,187.9	395
1975	1,012	76	162	1,117.0	416
1976	964	72	166	1,001.9	339
1977	987	122	116	1,103.8	290
1978	1,080	157	87	1,252.5	286
1979	1,027	122	85	1,365.8	323
1980	1,018	100	100	915.7	284
1981	985	73	130	1,460.2	248
1982	896	64	126	1,068.4	198
1983	829	63	76	828.9	173
1984	848	71	78	1,000.7	189
1985	852	59	102	1,550.9	226
1986	855	66	126	—	—
1987	874	64	127	—	—
1988	887	65	133	—	—

NOTE: See text for definition of variables and sources of data.

TABLE A-3   Selected Economic Indicators, Kenya, 1960-1988

Year	GDP (1985 U.S. dollars)	TT (index, 1980 = 100)	EXQ (index, 1980 = 100)	PPCOF (1985 U.S. dollars per ton)
1960	586	96	60	—
1961	516	93	67	455.2
1962	537	86	77	446.5
1963	565	91	82	381.5
1964	587	90	92	443.5
1965	586	88	93	451.2
1966	630	87	105	440.1
1967	649	78	106	388.1
1968	674	84	104	413.9
1969	695	73	130	399.6
1970	711	86	120	475.5
1971	884	87	112	504.4
1972	975	87	123	638.0
1973	933	88	137	635.6
1974	956	78	121	597.1
1975	936	74	115	529.5
1976	895	87	121	1,067.6
1977	937	118	124	1,551.4
1978	991	100	113	1,003.7
1979	981	95	105	932.2
1980	956	100	100	766.0
1981	917	93	92	557.2
1982	889	92	78	614.3
1983	850	88	86	700.5
1984	843	92	92	757.4
1985	845	91	83	690.4
1986	862	91	110	851.1
1987	883	73	100	583.2
1988	905	72	111	690.0

NOTE: See text for definition of variables and sources of data.

TABLE A-4   Selected Economic Indicators, Nigeria, 1960-1988

Year	GDP (1985 U.S. dollars)	TT (index, 1980 = 100)	EXQ (index, 1980 = 100)	PPCOC (1985 U.S. dollars per ton)
1960	951	18	38	—
1961	914	17	42	1,632.5
1962	914	16	43	1,560.5
1963	965	16	48	1,749.6
1964	1,000	16	52	1,936.2
1965	1,006	16	64	970.3
1966	932	15	71	1,171.4
1967	777	16	58	1,254.3
1968	766	16	50	1,385.8
1969	937	18	67	1,733.8
1970	1,150	19	85	1,712.2
1971	1,286	25	91	1,798.2
1972	1,306	23	106	1,840.5
1973	1,350	27	118	2,105.9
1974	1,471	57	119	2,375.9
1975	1,406	54	98	2,326.7
1976	1,492	57	126	2,051.3
1977	1,570	62	114	2,644.1
1978	1,488	53	97	2,647.8
1979	1,508	67	117	2,576.5
1980	1,499	100	100	2,845.5
1981	1,391	114	67	2,576.5
1982	1,343	107	56	2,284.6
1983	1,206	95	50	2,216.3
1984	1,065	95	58	2,070.7
1985	1,066	93	64	1,956.0
1986	1,057	51	48	4,222.2
1987	992	57	51	8,105.6
1988	995	45	56	8,590.0

NOTE: See text for definition of variables and sources of data.

TABLE A-5   Selected Economic Indicators, Senegal, 1960-1988

Year	GDP (1985 U.S. dollars)	TT (index, 1980 = 100)	EXQ (index 1980 = 100)	PPGN (1985 U.S. dollars per ton)	RAIN (millimeters in growing season, Diourbel)
1960	1,151	90	97	—	—
1961	1,173	90	120	—	144
1962	1,220	83	128	—	134
1963	1,255	80	119	—	107
1964	1,256	82	124	—	179
1965	1,261	87	122	—	143
1966	1,267	82	148	—	138
1967	1,239	87	126	414.7	175
1968	1,245	86	143	372.3	82
1969	1,110	94	109	343.8	176
1970	1,166	99	120	381.5	140
1971	1,153	101	90	449.9	164
1972	1,161	101	144	421.0	92
1973	1,098	85	124	436.7	83
1974	1,102	117	131	644.2	147
1975	1,158	128	131	566.3	124
1976	1,210	118	144	516.4	101
1977	1,200	136	151	504.7	83
1978	1,153	119	93	465.3	150
1979	1,211	102	130	470.0	117
1980	1,182	100	100	452.3	84
1981	1,155	108	101	589.2	—
1982	1,237	95	132	564.4	—
1983	1,215	90	143	491.6	—
1984	1,122	102	127	453.1	—
1985	1,156	102	132	498.7	—
1986	1,109	99	157	490.3	—
1987	1,115	96	146	480.3	—
1988	1,123	101	120	362.3	—

NOTE: See text for definition of variables and sources of data.

TABLE A-6   Selected Economic Indicators, Togo, 1960-1988

Year	GDP (1985 U.S. dollars)	TT (index, 1980 = 100)	EXQ (index, 1980 = 100)	PPCOC (1985 U.S. dollars per ton)	PPCOF (1985 U.S. dollars per ton)
1960	431	79	23	—	—
1961	422	69	34	—	—
1962	434	68	31	—	—
1963	429	68	32	1,381.9	1,480.6
1964	490	72	49	1,384.7	1,483.6
1965	579	69	45	885.6	1,549.8
1966	579	82	51	1,062.9	1,352.8
1967	624	77	47	1,409.1	1,509.7
1968	626	74	60	1,613.9	1,513.1
1969	664	79	64	1,679.8	1,431.6
1970	677	84	73	1,695.7	1,367.5
1971	671	80	63	1,553.2	1,252.6
1972	703	77	62	1,528.4	1,314.8
1973	708	77	61	1,554.3	1,472.5
1974	732	150	72	1,752.8	1,600.4
1975	713	161	41	1,217.9	1,167.2
1976	761	142	39	1,610.3	1,548.4
1977	824	101	72	1,519.5	1,468.8
1978	870	106	92	2,140.9	1,926.8
1979	821	89	84	2,330.7	2,118.8
1980	884	100	100	2,126.4	1,933.1
1981	818	91	72	1,883.8	1,800.1
1982	775	84	67	1,851.6	1,851.6
1983	690	81	67	1,852.7	1,953.7
1984	660	88	74	1,904.4	1,999.7
1985	665	87	75	1,755.2	1,941.3
1986	696	78	89	2,113.3	2,348.1
1987	658	63	123	1,925.6	2,139.5
1988	657	67	109	1,541.2	1,798.1

NOTE: See text for definition of variables and sources of data.

TABLE A-7   Selected Economic Indicators, Uganda, 1960-1988

Year	GDP (1985 U.S. dollars)	TT (index, 1980 = 100)	EXQ (index, 1980 = 100)	WBGDP (1980 U.S. dollars)
1960	228	87	177	—
1961	223	80	186	225
1962	226	78	190	214
1963	228	76	249	213
1964	234	79	284	220
1965	238	74	286	212
1966	251	84	264	216
1967	243	81	270	218
1968	241	83	260	216
1969	253	82	279	233
1970	250	91	299	227
1971	253	91	260	224
1972	248	82	290	221
1973	240	80	271	218
1974	240	68	242	215
1975	224	68	186	200
1976	224	93	182	199
1977	222	163	149	198
1978	203	104	128	180
1979	162	103	136	148
1980	154	100	100	137
1981	212	76	98	145
1982	343	75	145	159
1983	347	78	157	166
1984	396	97	128	151
1985	430	94	118	137
1986	—	108	106	125
1987	—	63	136	126
1988	—	63	117	—

NOTE: See text for definition of variables and sources of data.

TABLE A-8   World Commodity Prices, 1960-1987 (1980 U.S. dollars per unit)

Year	WPCOC	WPCOF	WPTEA	WPCOT	WPGN	WPPH	WPOIL
1960	205.20	194.40	495.50	226.50	—	45.30	6.60
1961	166.10	150.30	465.80	229.80	6.70	44.50	6.20
1962	154.60	160.30	463.30	221.20	5.75	38.70	6.10
1963	189.40	216.80	446.90	219.20	5.87	39.40	6.20
1964	169.50	269.50	444.60	215.40	6.26	42.00	6.00
1965	122.00	232.30	430.70	208.70	6.89	46.70	6.00
1966	166.60	241.20	404.20	194.90	6.00	41.80	5.80
1967	190.10	237.30	403.80	207.00	5.71	38.20	5.70
1968	231.10	242.30	334.90	215.40	5.32	36.90	5.80
1969	275.60	225.90	296.30	185.40	6.30	34.50	5.50
1970	193.40	265.30	314.00	181.10	6.54	31.50	5.20
1971	146.20	256.50	286.40	201.40	6.82	30.70	6.00
1972	161.00	247.50	263.00	198.30	6.35	28.80	6.30
1973	243.80	237.10	228.00	292.00	8.43	29.70	7.10
1974	276.30	229.00	248.10	250.40	13.08	96.50	17.00
1975	198.40	214.30	220.50	184.90	6.89	106.70	16.70
1976	321.20	441.60	241.30	265.50	6.64	56.50	18.10
1977	541.40	704.70	383.90	222.00	7.81	43.60	17.70
1978	422.70	403.90	271.90	195.30	7.84	36.00	15.80
1979	361.10	400.00	236.30	185.20	6.17	36.20	19.00
1980	260.40	324.40	223.10	204.70	4.86	46.70	29.40
1981	206.90	225.60	200.70	183.60	6.23	49.30	33.00
1982	175.21	247.20	195.00	161.12	3.87	42.74	34.27
1983	219.44	283.21	241.00	191.90	3.62	38.22	30.54
1984	252.47	321.02	364.43	188.10	3.69	40.31	30.54
1985	235.04	276.23	206.78	137.43	3.65	35.35	27.84
1986	182.54	286.16	170.02	93.12	—	30.25	11.90
1987	159.01	179.27	136.20	131.42	—	24.72	13.72

NOTE: See text for sources of data. WPCOC is real world price of cocoa; WPCOF is real world price of coffee; WPTEA is real world price of tea; WPCOT is real world price of cotton; WPGN is real world price of groundnuts; WPPH is real world price of phosphates; and WPOIL is real world price of crude petroleum.

B

Demographic and Health Surveys

The Demographic and Health Survey (DHS) Program began in 1984 with support from the United States Agency for International Development. The goal was to collect data on fertility, family planning, and maternal and child health. As of mid-1991, 36 surveys of women aged 15-49 had been carried out in Africa, Asia, and Latin America and the Caribbean, all in cooperation with local organizations. In the first phase of the program, which ended in 1990, surveys were conducted in twelve sub-Saharan African countries, including all but one of our seven study countries. The survey of Nigeria as a whole (as opposed to Ondo State, which was the site of an early survey) was completed as part of the second phase of DHS. Table B-1 presents the dates of the fieldwork and the sample sizes for each of the seven countries.

Women were asked the dates they entered into their first marital union and the dates their children were born, in terms of both the month and the year. They were also asked about the ages at which children had died. This information was generally collected in terms of days for deaths in the first month, months for deaths under 24 months, and years otherwise. We have converted the information on age at death into estimates of the date of death in terms of months. The women were also asked about their own socioeconomic characteristics, such as the highest level of school attended, religion, and ethnicity.

DHS undertook an analysis of the quality of the data collected in part of the first phase of its program, including the surveys in Botswana, Ghana, Senegal, Togo, and Uganda (Institute for Resource Development, 1990). It

TABLE B-1 Date and Sample Size of the Demographic and
Health Surveys in the Seven Study Countries

Country	Dates of Fieldwork	Sample Size
Botswana	August-December 1988	4,368
Ghana	February-May 1988	4,488
Kenya	December 1988-May 1989	7,150
Nigeria	April-October 1990	8,781
Senegal	April-July 1986	4,415
Togo	June-November 1988	3,360
Uganda	September 1988-February 1989	4,730

SOURCE: Institute for Resource Development (1991).

found some misrecording of women's ages at the very youngest and oldest ages, so that the women would not be eligible for a full interview, but overall found that fertility would be overestimated as a result by only about 4 percent in some of the African surveys (Rutstein and Bicego, 1990). Not all women were able to report the month and year they formed their first union; the problem increased with the age of the woman (Blanc and Rutenberg, 1990). However, in most countries women could report at least the year of first marriage or the age at which they were first married, so that the year of marriage could be imputed. Information was lacking for no more than 2 percent of women in Botswana, Ghana, and Senegal, and for fewer than 1 percent in Togo and Uganda. Misreporting of union dates seems to have been greatest in Togo.

Ninety-nine percent of women were able to give at least the calendar year, if not the month, of the births of their children or their own age at the time (Arnold, 1990). Reliance on information on age of mother at time of birth was greatest in Togo, where for 31 percent of the children the year and month of birth had to be imputed on that basis. There is also some concern that births were displaced to longer than five years before the survey, so that information on health, breastfeeding, and family planning related to these births would not have to be collected.

Data on the age at death of children were 98 to 100 percent complete in the five of our study countries considered (Sullivan et al., 1990). Some evidence suggests age heaping, most notably for Ghana, which we have tried to address in our analysis by avoiding heaping points in defining age groups. Mortality data were also analyzed by characteristics of the mother and child to ascertain possible data problems. For Botswana, there may have been some underreporting of neonatal deaths, especially among first-born females born to young mothers. There may also have been some systematic omission of births in the Botswana survey (Hill, 1992). Information on child survival from the Kenya DHS also suggests some omission of dead children, particularly for more distant time periods (Working Group on Kenya, 1993).

One source of error not systematically investigated by the DHS data quality exercise that might have a substantial effect on the analysis in this report is the reported timing of events. The DHS evaluation gives some indication that births may have been intentionally moved backward in time to locate them before the cutoff date for additional questions about recent births and young children. Other time location errors could include the reporting of an event as occurring at some round number of months or years ago (digital preference), as well as the systematic mislocation of events, such as was found in some of the World Fertility Surveys (Brass and Rashad, 1981). Digital preference would lead to surpluses and deficits of events in particular years, but might be expected to be distributed randomly with respect to economic variables, especially since the surveys were taken in different years. Bias in reporting timing, that is wholesale shifts of events to earlier or later periods, would be more likely to affect estimates of underlying trend than short-term fluctuations, so the possible existence of such bias in the DHS surveys used here argues for caution in interpreting the trend estimates reported in Chapters 5 and 6. The distortion of trends estimated from retrospectively reported events might be largest for marriages, since not only might the date be misreported, but the nature of the event (the process by which a union is formed) might itself change (van de Walle, 1993).

In summary, the quality of the data was remarkably good, although the problems for the nine sub-Saharan African surveys analyzed for that purpose by DHS were generally greater than those for surveys in other regions of the world.

References

Allison, P.D.
  1982   Discrete-time methods for the analysis of event histories. Pp. 61-98 in S. Leinhardt, ed., *Sociological Methodology*. San Francisco: Jossey-Bass.

Arnold, F.
  1990   Assessment of the quality of birth history data in the Demographic and Health Surveys. Pp. 81-111 in *An Assessment of DHS-I Data Quality*. DHS Methodological Reports, No. 1. Columbia, Md.: Institute for Resource Development/ Macro Systems, Inc.

Ashton, B., K. Hill, A. Piazza, and R. Zeitz
  1984   Famine in China, 1958-61. *Population and Development Review* 10(4):613-646.

Azam, J.P., and T. Besley
  1989   The supply of manufactured goods and agricultural development: The case of Ghana. *OECD Development Centre Paper*. Paris: Organisation for Economic Co-operation and Development.

Banque Centrale des Etats de l'Afrique de l'Ouest
  var.   *Notes d'Information et Statistiques*. Dakar.
  iss.

Bienen, H.
  1983   Income distribution and politics in Nigeria. Pp. 85-104 in I. W. Zartman, ed., *The Political Economy of Nigeria*. New York: Praeger.

Blanc, A.K., and N. Rutenberg
  1990   Assessment of the quality of data on age at first sexual intercourse, age at first marriage, and age at first birth in the Demographic and Health Surveys. Pp. 39-79 in *An Assessment of DHS-I Data Quality*. DHS Methodological Reports, No. 1. Columbia, Md.: Institute for Resource Development/Macro Systems, Inc.

Brass, W., and H. Rashad
  1981   Evaluation of levels and trends in fertility from WFS data: Bangladesh. In M.R. Khan, ed., *Fertility and Mortality Trends in Bangladesh*. Dacca: Bangladesh Institute of Development Studies.

Bravo, J.
1992   Economic crises and mortality: Short and medium-term changes in Latin America. Paper prepared for the International Union for the Scientific Study of Population Peopling of the Americas Conference, Veracruz, Mexico, May 18-22.

Brenner, M.H.
1973   Fetal, infant, and maternal mortality during periods of economic instability. *International Journal of Health Services* 3(2):145-159.
1983   Mortality and economic instability: Detailed analyses for Britain and comparative analyses for selected industrialized countries. *International Journal of Health Services* 13(4):563-620.
1987   Economic change, alcohol consumption and heart disease mortality in nine industrialized countries. *Social Science and Medicine* 25(2):119-132.

Butz, W.F., and M.P. Ward
1979   The emergence of countercyclical U.S. fertility. *American Economic Review* 69:319-328.

Caldwell, J.C.
1986   Periodic high risk as a cause of fertility decline in a changing rural environment: Survival strategies in the 1980-1983 South Indian drought. *Economic Development and Cultural Change* 34(4):677-703.
1987   Cultural context of high fertility in sub-Saharan Africa. *Population and Development Review* 13(3):409-437.

Caldwell, J.C., and P. Caldwell
1987   Famine in Africa. Paper presented at the International Union for the Scientific Study of Population Seminar on Mortality in Society in Sub-Saharan Africa, Yaoundé, Cameroon, October 19-23.
1990   High fertility in sub-Saharan Africa. *Scientific American* May:118-125.

Caldwell, J.C., I.O. Orubuloye, and P. Caldwell
1992   Fertility decline in Africa: A new type of transition? *Population and Development Review* 18(2):211-242.

Central Bank of Nigeria
var.   *Annual Report and Statement of Accounts.* Lagos.
yrs.

Central Intelligence Agency
1989   *The World Factbook.* Washington, D.C.

Coale, A.J.
1984   *Rapid Population Change in China, 1952-1982.* Committee on Population and Demography, Report No. 27. Washington, D.C.: National Academy Press.

Cohen, B.
1993   Fertility levels, differentials, and trends. In K.A. Foote, K.H. Hill, and L.G. Martin, eds., *Demographic Change in Sub-Saharan Africa.* Panel on the Population Dynamics of Sub-Saharan Africa, Committee on Population, National Research Council. Washington, D.C.: National Academy Press.

Cornia, G.A., R. Jolly, and F. Stewart, eds.
1987   *Adjustment with a Human Face: Protecting the Vulnerable and Promoting Growth.* Oxford: Clarendon Press.
1989   *Adjustment with a Human Face: Country Case Studies.* Oxford: Clarendon Press.

Crafts, N.F.R.
1983   Gross national product in Europe 1870-1910: Some new estimates. *Explorations in Economic History* 20:387-401.

Diop, F.
    1990   Economic determinants of child health and utilization of health services in sub-
            Saharan Africa: The case of Ivory Coast. Ph.D. dissertation, The Johns Hopkins
            University.
Easterlin, R.A.
    1965   Long swings in U.S. demographic and economic growth: Some findings on the
            historical pattern. *Demography* 2:490-507.
Federal Office of Statistics, Nigeria, and Institute for Resource Development
    1992   *Nigeria Demographic and Health Survey 1990.* Columbia, Md.: Institute for
            Resource Development/Macro International, Inc.
Food and Agriculture Organization
    1983   *FAO Production Yearbook* 37. Rome.
Foster, A., J. Menken, A. Chowdhury, and J. Trussell
    1986   Female reproductive development: A hazards model analysis. *Social Biology*
            33(3-4):183-198.
Galloway, P.
    1988   Basic patterns in annual variations in fertility, nuptiality, mortality, and prices in
            pre-industrial Europe. *Population Studies* 42(2):275-302.
Gersovitz, M.
    1986   Agro-Industrial processing and agricultural processing under uncertainty. *Review
            of Economic Studies* 53:153-169.
    1987   Some sources and implications of uncertainty in the Senegalese economy. Pp. 15-
            46 in J. Waterbury and M. Gersovitz, eds., *The Political Economy of Risk and
            Choice in Senegal.* London: Frank Cass and Co.
Gersovitz, M., and C.H. Paxson
    1990   *The Economies of Africa and the Prices of their Exports.* Princeton Studies in
            International Finance, Number 68. Princeton, N.J.
Godfrey, M.
    1986   *Kenya to 1990: Prospects for Growth.* London: Economist Intelligence Unit.
Heckman, J.J., and J.R. Walker
    1990   The relationship between wages and income and the timing and spacing of births.
            Econometrica 58(6):1411-1441.
Hesp, P.
    1985   *Producer Prices in Tropical Africa: A Review of Official Prices for Tropical
            Africa: 1960-1980.* African Studies Centre Research Report No. 23, Leiden.
Hicks, N., and A. Kubisch
    1984   Cutting government revenues in LDCs. *Finance and Development* 21(Septem-
            ber):37-39.
Hill, A.L.L.
    1993   Trends in childhood mortality. In K.A. Foote, K.H. Hill, and L.G. Martin, eds.,
            Demographic Change in Sub-Saharan Africa. Panel on the Population Dynamics
            of Sub-Saharan Africa, Committee on Population, National Research Council. Wash-
            ington, D.C.: National Academy Press.
Hill, C.B., and D.N. Mokgethi
    1989   Botswana: Macroeconomic management of commodity booms. Pp. 174-206 in
            *Successful Development in Africa: Case Studies of Projects, Programs, and Poli-
            cies.* Washington, D.C.: The World Bank.
Hill, K.H.
    1991   Demographic response to economic shock. *Working Paper WPS* 652. Policy,
            Research and External Affairs, World Development Report. Washington, D.C.:
            The World Bank.

1992   Scope and methodology. Pp. 12-15 in *Child Mortality Since the 1960s: A Database for Developing Countries.* New York: United Nations.

Hill, K.H., and A. Palloni

1992   Demographic responses to economic shocks: The case of Latin America. Paper prepared for the International Union for the Scientific Study of Population Peopling of the Americas Conference, Veracruz, Mexico, May 18-22.

Hill, K.H., and A.R. Pebley

1989   Child mortality in the developing world. *Population and Development Review* 15(4):657-687.

Hobcraft, J.N., J.W. McDonald, and S.O. Rutstein

1985   Demographic determinants of infant and early child mortality: A comparative analysis. *Population Studies* 39(3):363-385.

Institute for Resource Development

1990   *An Assessment of DHS-I Data Quality.* DHS Methodological Reports, No. 1. Columbia, Md.: Institute for Resource Development/Macro Systems, Inc.

1991   *Demographic and Health Surveys Newsletter* 4(1):6-7.

var.   *Demographic and Health Surveys.* Columbia, Md.: Institute for

yrs.   Resource Development/Macro Systems, Inc.

International Labour Organization

var.   *Yearbook of Labour Statistics.* Geneva.

yrs.

International Monetary Fund

1987   *International Financial Statistics* (data tape). Washington, D.C.

Jolly, C.L., and J.N. Gribble

1993   The proximate determinants of fertility. In K.A. Foote, K.H. Hill, and L.G. Martin, eds., *Demographic Change in Sub-Saharan Africa.* Panel on the Population Dynamics of Sub-Saharan Africa, Committee on Population, National Research Council. Washington, D.C.: National Academy Press.

Jolly, R., and G.A. Cornia, eds.

1984   *The Impact of World Recession on Children.* Oxford: Pergamon Press.

Kenya Central Bureau of Statistics

var.   *Statistical Abstract.* Nairobi.

yrs.

Killick, T.

1978   *Development Economics in Action: A Study of Economic Policies in Ghana.* New York: St. Martins Press.

Kirk-Greene, A., and D. Rimmer

1981   *Nigeria Since 1970: A Political and Economic Outline.* London: Hodder and Stoughton.

Lee, R.D.

1981   Short-term variation: Vital rates, prices and weather. Pp. 356-401 in E.A. Wrigley and R.W. Schofield, eds., *The Population History of England 1541-1871: A Reconstruction.* Cambridge, Mass.: Harvard University.

1990   The demographic response to economic crisis in historical and contemporary populations. *Population Bulletin of the United Nations* 29:1-15.

Lindauer, D.L., O.A. Meesook, and P. Suebsaeng

1988   Government wage policy in Africa: Some findings and policy issues. *World Bank Research Observer* 3(1):1-25.

Mata, L.

1985   Estado nutricional del niño de Puriscal durante la crisis, 1979-1984. *Revista Médica del Hospital Nacional de Niños de Costa Rica* 20(2):121-140.

1987   A public health approach to the "food-malnutrition-economic recession" complex. In D. Bell and M. Reich, eds., *Health, Nutrition and Economic Crisis: Approaches to Policy in the Third World.* Westport, Conn.: Auburn House (Greenwood).

McAvinchey, I.D., and A. Wagstaff
1987   Distributed lags in the relationship between unemployment and mortality: The case of the United Kingdom. *Department of Economics Discussion Paper* 87-21. Aberdeen, Scotland: University of Aberdeen.

Menken, J., J. Trussell, and S. Watkins
1981   The nutrition fertility link: An evaluation of the evidence. *Journal of Interdisciplinary History* XI(3):425-441.

Murphy, M.
1992   Economic models of fertility in post-war Britain—A conceptual and statistical reinterpretation. *Population Studies* 46:235-258.

Neter, J., and W. Wasserman
1974   *Applied Linear Statistical Models.* Homewood, Ill.: Richard D. Irwin.

Ogbu, O., and M. Gallagher
1992   Public expenditures and health care in Africa. *Social Science and Medicine* 34(6):615-624.

Palloni, A., and M. Tienda
1991   Demographic responses to economic recessions in Latin America since 1900. *Sociological Inquiry* 62:246-270.

Panel on the Population Dynamics of Sub-Saharan Africa
1993   *Demographic Change in Sub-Saharan Africa*, K.A. Foote, K.H. Hill, and L.G. Martin, eds. Committee on Population, National Research Council. Washington, D.C.: National Academy Press.

Preston, S.H.
1980   Causes and consequences of mortality declines in less developed countries during the twentieth century. Pp. 289-360 in R.A. Easterlin, ed., *Population and Economic Change in Developing Countries.* Chicago: University of Chicago.

Ravallion, M.
1987   *Markets and Famines.* Oxford: Clarendon Press.

Razzaque, A., N. Alam, L. Wai, and A. Foster
1990   Sustained effects of the 1974-75 famine on infant and child mortality in a rural area of Bangladesh. *Population Studies* 44:145-154.

Rosenzweig, M.
1988   Risk, private information, and the family. *American Economic Review* 78(2):245-250.

Rutstein, S.O., and G.T. Bicego
1990   Assessment of the quality of data used to ascertain eligibility and age in the Demographic and Health Surveys. Pp. 3-37 in *An Assessment of DHS-I Data Quality.* DHS Methodological Reports, No. 1. Columbia, Md.: Institute for Resource Development/Macro Systems, Inc.

Saadah, F.
1991   Socioeconomic determinants of child survival in Ghana: Evidence from Living Standards Measurement Survey 1987-88. Ph.D. dissertation, The Johns Hopkins University.

Stein, Z., M. Susser, G. Saenger, and F. Marolla
1975   *Famine and Human Development: The Dutch Hunger Winter of 1944-45.* New York: Oxford University Press.

Sullivan, J.M., G.T. Bicego, and S.O. Rutstein
1990   Assessment of the quality of data used for the direct estimation of infant and child

mortality in the Demographic and Health Surveys. Pp. 113-137 in *An Assessment of DHS-1 Data Quality*. DHS Methodological Reports, No. 1. Columbia, Md.: Institute for Resource Development/Macro Systems, Inc.

Summers, R., and A. Heston
  1991   The Penn World Table (Mark 5): An expanded set of international comparisons, 1950-88. *Quarterly Journal of Economics* CVI(2):327-368.

Taucher, E.
  1989   Behavioral factors in demographic responses to economic crises. Paper prepared for the International Union for the Scientific Study of Population XXIst International Population Conference, New Delhi, September 20-27.

Tostensen, A., and J.G. Scott
  1987   *Kenya: Country Study and Norwegian Aid Review*. Fantoft, Norway: Chr. Michelsen Institute.

Trussell, J., and T. Guinnane
  1993   Techniques of event history analysis. In D. Reher and R. Schofield, eds., *Old and New Methods in Historical Demography*. Oxford: Clarendon Press.

United Nations
  1991   *World Population and Prospects 1990*. New York.

United Nations Committee on Trade and Development
  var.   *Handbook of International Trade and Development*. Geneva.
  iss.

United Nations Development Program/World Bank
  1989   *African Economic and Financial Data* (book and data diskettes). Washington, D.C.: The World Bank.

U.S. Department of the Interior
  1984   *Mineral Industries of Africa*. Washington, D.C.

Vandemoortele, J.
  1991   Labour market informalisation in sub-Saharan Africa. Pp. 81-113 in G. Standing and V. Tokman, eds., *Towards Social Adjustment: Labour Market Issues in Structural Adjustment*. Geneva: International Labour Office.

van de Walle, E.
  1993   Recent trends in marriage ages. In K.A. Foote, K.H. Hill, and L.G. Martin, eds., *Demographic Change in Sub-Saharan Africa*. Panel on the Population Dynamics of Sub-Saharan Africa, Committee on Population, National Research Council. Washington, D.C.: National Academy Press.

Vaupel, J., A. Yashin, and K.G. Manton
  1988   Debilitation's aftermath: Stochastic process models of mortality. *Mathematical Population Studies* 1(2):21-48.

Watts, M., and P. Lubeck
  1983   The popular classes and the oil boom: A political economy of rural and urban poverty. Pp. 105-144 in W. Zartman, ed., *The Political Economy of Nigeria*. New York: Praeger.

Working Group on Kenya
  1993   *Demographic Change in Kenya*, W. Brass and C.L. Jolly, eds. Panel on the Population Dynamics of Sub-Saharan Africa, Committee on Population, National Research Council. Washington, D.C.: National Academy Press.

World Bank
  1981   *World Development Report, 1981*. Washington, D.C.
  1983   *Kenya: Growth and Structural Change*. Washington, D.C.
  1986a   *Commodity Trade and Price Trends*. Washington, D.C.
  1986b   *World Development Report, 1986*. Washington, D.C.

1989a   *Ghana: Population, Health and Nutrition Sector Review.* Washington, D.C.
1989b   *Sub-Saharan Africa: From Crisis to Sustainable Growth.* Washington, D.C.
1991   *Trends in Developing Economies.* Washington, D.C.

Younger, S.D.
1989   Ghana: Economic recovery program, a case study of stabilization and structural adjustment in sub-Saharan Africa. Pp. 128-173 in *Successful Development in Africa: Case Studies of Projects, Programs, and Policies.* Washington, D.C.: The World Bank.